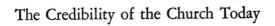

The Credibility of the Church Today

The Credibility
of the Church Today

A Reply to Charles Davis

Gregory Baum

HERDER AND HERDER

1968
HERDER AND HERDER NEW YORK
232 Madison Avenue, New York 10016

Nihil obstat: Leo J. Steady, Censor Librorum
Imprimatur: ✠ Robert F. Joyce, Bishop of Burlington
March 26, 1968

Contents

To My Colleagues in the Faculty of Theology
at St. Michael's College, in the University of Toronto

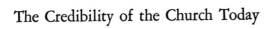

The Credibility of the Church Today

Introduction

CHARLES Davis has left the Catholic Church. In his *A Question of Conscience* he explains why the self-understanding of the Catholic Church is no longer credible to him. He offers essentially two sets of reasons. First he tries to show that the traditional arguments in favour of the Catholic claims have lost their validity. Using a similar kind of logic, he attempts to prove that the Catholic Church as institution has become a counter-sign of the Gospel. According to him, the institutional Church signifies today the absence of Christ. Secondly Charles Davis attempts to show that the evolution of man's self-understanding has produced a new ideal of social organization and that, as a consequence of this, all the Christian Churches are moving toward total dissolution. The future of the Gospel lies with the believing people. They shall construct flexible social organizations which are demanded as the expression of their evolving social life.

While I have much sympathy for the complaints Charles Davis raises against the Catholic Church and I agree with most of the descriptions he gives of the present state of affairs, I have a totally different interpretation of what is actually taking place in the Catholic Church. Since Charles Davis has asked Catholic theologians to reply to his reflections and explain why the Catholic Church continues to make sense to them, I wish to discuss the

11

issue of the Church's credibility today and develop arguments that bring out the meaningfulness of the Church in the present age.

The crucial difference between Davis and myself lies in the evaluation of Vatican II. I regard Vatican II as an extraordinary institutional event in the life of the Catholic Church. I look upon Vatican II as the beginning—or at least, with Karl Rahner, as the beginning of the beginning—of a profound doctrinal reform in the Catholic Church. A careful study reveals that the doctrinal development at Vatican II is much more startling than a casual reading of the conciliar documents suggests.

The most important doctrinal shift that will occupy us in this book is the clear affirmation of God's redemptive involvement in all of human history. God is present to human life. Or, to use scholastic terminology, human life is supernatural. Since the end of man is one and supernatural the dynamics of human life and history must also be regarded as supernatural. There is no neutral ground between sin and grace. While traditional theology has always admitted this, Vatican II has placed this at the centre of its teaching, especially in the *Pastoral Constitution on the Church in the Modern World,* and produced what must be called a doctrinal shift. We may speak of the new teaching of Vatican II.

Even people who are not particularly interested in religion know that the Vatican Council has made significant changes in Catholic life. It has changed the relationship of Catholics with other people—with other Christians, with Jews, with members of other religions, and even with men not interested in religion at all. People usually know that at Vatican II the Catholic Church has approved of dialogue, dialogue with others, dialogue within the Church, and—by changing the language of the liturgy—dialogue of God's Word and man's response. The ordinary observers of the Church are not misled. These changes are indeed highly significant developments. The dogmatic basis on which they occurred is the new understanding of man: human life, everywhere, is the realization of a dialogue of salvation with God. The teaching of Vatican II has shifted, or at least begun to shift, the focal point of the Gospel. The Good News is the divine message about human life. Good News is that God is redemptively involved wherever people are. In a book which I began last spring and hope to conclude in the course of this year, I am examining in detail the origin and meaning of this doctrinal shift and its theological and practical implications. The re-focusing of the Gospel that has begun to take place at Vatican II has a profound effect on the Catholic understanding of Church, of faith and sacraments, and even of the saving, transcendent reality we call God. I believe that the doctrinal shift that occurred at Vatican II enables the Church to deal with a central problem, namely the conceptualization of divine transcendence in harmony with the Scriptures and in keeping with man's contemporary experience of reality.

The doctrinal movement which found—in part at least—institutional expression at Vatican II began at the end of the 19th century with the writings of Maurice Blondel.[1] Blondel was the first to acknowledge that the modern experience of reality demanded a re-thinking of the problem of God. He was the first to realize that the historical character of human life, brought out by philosophy, psychology, and the entire intellectual experience of the West, gave the Christian theologian a better possibility of expressing God's presence to human life than did the more static understanding of man, characteristic of the past. While traditional theologians also affirmed God's involvement in human life, it was Maurice Blondel, steering his way between modernists and veterists, who made the gratuitous saving presence of God to human life the focal point of his understanding of the Christian creed. The message of Jesus Christ makes known to men the hidden, redemptive involvement of God wherever people are.

Maurice Blondel has had little influence on the official theology taught at Catholic seminaries. Yet in dialogue with him and wrestling with the same issues of modern life many of the creative theologians of the Catholic Church acknowledged the new focus of the Gospel, —even if they expressed themselves in different sets of concepts. Good News is that God is redemptively present wherever people are. The most famous contemporary author who has placed this theme at the centre of his doctrinal synthesis, drawn out many of its hidden theological implications and defended the relevance of the Church in a redemptive humanity, is Karl Rahner.[2] At Vatican II this theological movement had sufficient influence to assure that the Blondelian perspective was, if not adopted consistently, then at least affirmed in several conciliar documents, especially in the *Pastoral Constitution on the Church in the Modern World*.

I regard the impact of Maurice Blondel, with his non-Aristotelian epistemology and anthropology, as a turning point in the history of the Catholic Church comparable to, though exceeding in proportion, the entry of Aristotelian categories in the Church through the great scholastics of the 13th century. After considerable shock the new Aristotelian categories—especially that of the *natura humana,* defined by genus and specific difference and constituted by the four causes—influenced the thinking in the Church, entered the teaching of the ecclesiastical authorities, and determined the Church's legislation and the forms of her social life. In the present century the impact of Maurice Blondel and the movement promoting his central insight have produced an even greater shock. At Vatican II the Blondelian perspective has been adopted, at least in part, in the authoritative teaching of the Catholic Church.

It is no accident that the *Pastoral Constitution on the Church in the Modern World* no longer employs the distinction between natural and supernatural. It acknowledges throughout the Blondelian perspective that God is graciously present in the dynamics of human life and history. Man is always more than man. I think that in essence the old concept of the *natura humana* has been overcome in the conciliar teaching, even if the documents do not draw all the consequences of this deepening of the perspective. The entire moral teaching of the Church based on the concept of the *natura humana,* defined by genus and specific difference, is inadequate. The present crisis in regard to birth control is just one instance of this inadequacy. None of the official positions, based on a fixed *natura humana,* which are so rigidly defended at this time—be they concerned with marriage, sex, property, war, and so forth—will remain with us for long. In essence they have been overcome in the doctrinal development at Vatican II.

The present upheaval in the Church and the doctrinal uncertainty so widely spread are, according to my view, signs of the gradual process of re-interpreting the entire teaching of the Church in the light of the new focus. Vatican II began this in a few instances. In a process in which dialogue and some conflict are essential the Catholic Church remains faithful to the Word spoken to her in the past and addressing her in the present, by proclaiming divine revelation, infallibly held by her in faith, as the Good News for the contemporary age.

Charles Davis was deeply moved by the birth control crisis. So was I. A number of years ago I publicly disagreed with the

15

official position of the Holy See.[3] There are conditions under which it is moral and licit for a loyal Catholic to disagree with an official position dealing with human wisdom and human values. In the present day as we are shifting from a static to a more dynamic, historical understanding of man—in whose history sin and God's saving action are involved—these conditions are given rather frequently. Catholics are learning to make up their own minds in responsible fashion. However, what is tragic and, perhaps, immoral is that these official positions, based on a fixed *natura humana,* still determine the public policies of some governments in regard to population problems and other issues touching upon the well-being of millions of people. The number of Catholics is growing who regard the papal insistence on the right to decide these matters for the entire Church and her bishops as an abuse of legitimate and divinely given authority. But this does not make the Catholic Church meaningless.

The temptation to regard the Church as meaningless comes to me from seeing the overwhelming powers of evil that pervade human life. Have we not totally failed in discerning this evil? Have we not been blind to the awful things that have happened, and still happen in our midst? Have we not been silent when millions of Jews were exterminated? Have we not missed the demonic powers implicit in nationalism which are leading us to repeated and more extended conflagrations? What is meaningful in such a world? It is certainly not meaningful, one wants to say, to quibble about the Churches, to argue about true or false doctrines, to quarrel about the eucharistic presence or valid ministry, when all of them together have kept us blind to the destructive forces in life and do not enable us now to resist them.

Yet faith means to believe that evil is not the only force at work in the human situation. The Good News is that God is graciously present to human life. Wherever people are they are summoned to enter more deeply into their humanity; wherever people are they are called to move forward to their destiny. This is the message of Jesus. Man is always more than man. Man is never totally left to the destructive tendencies that qualify his situation. In the power of the Spirit God is at work in human life: he summons and graces men to become more conformed to the perfect manhood that is in Jesus Christ. The Church is the community of men who believe that there is hope.

Before dealing with the issue of credibility, raised by Charles Davis, therefore, I must present the doctrine of the Church as a message of hope for all men.

1.

The Open Church

AT the Second Vatican Council a significant development occurred in the self-understanding of the Catholic Church. Listening to the Word of God and responding to the tested experience
of the Christian community, the Council has—cautiously perhaps,
but nonetheless clearly—given expression to a new way of understanding the mystery of Church.

It has become increasingly difficult for Christians today to
understand the mystery of Church simply in terms of the ecclesiastical community. We find it almost impossible to regard
the Gospel of Christ as a charter of privilege for a limited group
of people. Unless the story of salvation tells us who are other
people and what is their destiny, it becomes a stumbling
block for the present generation. Since we regard it as one of our
greatest temptations to be exclusively concerned with ourselves
and our own group, we shy away from an understanding of the
Gospel that would confirm us in the self-centredness and group-
egotism that come to us so naturally. In the present age man's
preoccupation with his own is a destructive factor that threatens
to destroy the world. What we have to learn over and over again

is to include others in our own concern. Only if we make progress on this road will the human family have a future in this world. Since we believe that Christ is the universal saviour we look for an understanding of the Gospel that illumines the situation of mankind and enables us to become brothers to all men. We hope that the mystery of Church, which sums up what God does for mankind in Christ, tells us not simply what God is doing among Christians but what he is doing in the entire human family. Many Christians today will accept a doctrine on the Church only if it becomes a key for the understanding of the whole human community.

Prior to the Vatican Council ecclesiastical teaching and the common theological tradition formulated the mystery of Church in exclusivist or restrictive terms.[1] It was taught that the communion which God creates among Christians is restricted to the Church. Men beyond the boundaries of the Church are excluded from this Spirit-created fellowship. *Extra ecclesiam nulla salus.*[2] When we said Church, we divided the human race into two categories, Catholics and non-Catholics. Catholic teaching did not necessarily deny that other people could be saved or that Christians separated from the Church could be hidden with Christ in God, but Catholics regarded the saving action of God outside the Church as the unexpected, as an exception to the order established by him, and hence would not let God's worldwide saving action influence their understanding of the Church.[3]

This restrictive or closed understanding of Church dominated almost the entire life of the Church. It affected the outlook of Catholics on other people and determined ecclesiastical legislation—for instance, on common worship or mixed marriages. It had a distinctive effect on the social environment to which Catholics belonged.

It should hardly be necessary to add that the ecclesiastical teachers and theologians who proposed this restrictive notion of Church were not unenlightened or hard-hearted men. It seems to me that a theory of doctrinal development which assumes that Christians are holier today than they were in the past cannot stand up. The restrictive understanding of Church was proposed by men who wanted to be faithful to divine revelation and who understood the Scriptures in the light of their Christian experience. The traditional teaching was a source of assurance and consolation for Catholics. It proposed the teaching of Christ to people who only knew societies in which the lines of demarcation were clearly drawn.

This venerable theological and ecclesiastical tradition was changed at Vatican II.[4] The doctrine of the Church, as proposed in the conciliar documents—cautiously, perhaps, but clearly nonetheless—tell us the significant truth about all men. It reveals to us the mystery of new life, present in the whole of the human community. It enables us to enter into solidarity with all men and, at the same time, to belong to a special, visible people in the world.

THE MEANING OF "CHURCH"

The Vatican Council refused to define what the Church is and then use this word consistently throughout the documents with the identical meaning. We shall examine the different ways in which the word "Church" is used in the conciliar documents.

First, "Church" is equated with Catholic Church. The Christian people united by Catholic teaching, the sevenfold sacramental liturgy, and the acknowledgement of papal and collegial authority—this is what the conciliar documents, following the traditional teaching, call Church. The Catholic Church regards herself as the Church of Christ in a unique sense. What this means we shall see in a later chapter.

"Church", secondly, refers to the local congregation.[5] One of the great achievements of the Vatican Council was the recovery of a theology of the local Church. We are repeatedly told that through the celebration of the Word and the eucharistic meal Christ is present in the worshipping community and, in the power of the Spirit, transforms it into his body.[6] The Church of Christ is present in the local congregations and hence these congregations gathered at worship are rightfully called Churches. More specifically, "Church" is the name given to the gathering of local congregations in the unity of a diocese or an episcopally governed ecclesiastical community. Here, too, the Church of Christ is present. Because of the unity of truth and ministry in the bishop, the entire Church, one holy, catholic, and apostolic is present in episcopally governed Churches. The conciliar documents refer to them as local or particular Churches. The local Churches, we are told, are fashioned in the image of the Church; they unite many local congregations in the unity of a single Church. The Catholic Church, according to the conciliar documents, is not understood as an administrative union of the local Churches under a supreme ecclesiastical government, but as a body or family of local Churches which constitute the Church universal and in which it exists.

There is no need, for our purpose, to analyze more carefully the notion of local Church.

"Church", thirdly, refers to the community of the baptised. *The Constitution on the Church* tells us that the baptism of faith constitutes men as a spiritual house and a holy priesthood,[7] and the

Decree on Ecumenism says that baptism properly celebrated incorporates believers into Christ and constitutes "the sacramental bond of unity existing among all who through it are reborn."[8] There are obstacles to Christian unity, but "in spite of them it remains true that all who have been justified by faith in baptism are incorporated into Christ; they therefore have a right to be called Christians and with good reason are accepted as brothers by the children of the Catholic Church".[9] Christians, then, are brothers. There exists a Spirit-created sacramental communion between Catholics and other Christians, even if a dimension of this communion is incomplete.[10] Church, then, may refer to this sacramental fellowship created by faith and baptism.

When the conciliar documents oppose "Church" and humanity, they usually signify by Church the community created by the baptismal covenant in contrast to the greater part of mankind, that is not baptized. This appears in the first paragraph of the *Pastoral Constitution on the Church in the Modern World:* "The joys and the hopes, the griefs and the anxieties of the men of this age, especially those who are poor or in any way afflicted, these too are the joys and the hopes, the griefs and the anxieties of the followers of Christ. Indeed nothing genuinely human fails to raise an echo in their hearts. For theirs is a community composed of men. United in Christ, they are led by the Holy Spirit in the journey to the kingdom of their Father and they have welcomed the news of salvation which is meant for every man. That is why this community realizes that it is truly and intimately linked with mankind and its history." The Church here is the community of the followers of Christ.

In this context we note that the Vatican Council refers to the other Christian Churches of East and West as "Churches" and affirms, with varying qualifications, their ecclesial character[11]

The Catholic Church here acknowledges that other Christian Churches are communities in which Christ is present and instruments of the Spirit in saving and sanctifying men. This in itself, we observe, is a remarkable doctrinal development.

"Church", fourthly, refers to the people of Israel. The people of the old covenant, chosen by God to give witness to him among the nations, are called his congregation, his *ecclesia,* his Church.[12] The reality signified by the word "Church", therefore, does not begin with Jesus and the community of his followers. The roots of the Church lie in the past. The Church as the community of the new covenant is in continuity—continuity combining promise and fulfilment—with the people of the old covenant. God revealed himself in view of his total self-communication in Christ, in the liberation of Israel from the land of bondage and the creation of a consecrated people in the desert. According to the biblical story, the roots of the Church reach even beyond Moses to the distant past, described as the age of the patriarchs. It was already in Abraham, chosen by God to become the father of a great nation, that the history of salvation, culminating in Jesus Christ, had its beginning. In Abraham's election the entire Church participates.[13] The ancient patriarch, of which the Scriptures say that he was justified by faith, is the father of the faithful. In the words of the liturgy, he is "our father in faith". Church, therefore, is the entire Abrahamic community, the community of the called, beginning with Abraham and stretching through history.

We note in this connection the significant doctrinal development that took place at Vatican II in spelling out the relation between the people of Israel today and the Christian Church. The Jewish people as the community of the faithful is here acknowledged as "the people of election, most dear to God

because of [his promises to] their fathers".[14] The acknowledgement of God's fidelity to Israel and the presence of his living
Word in the faithful community—according to the intimations
of the apostole Paul—represents one of those doctrinal developments which, while faithful to the Scriptures, must impress the
historian of doctrine as something of a discontinuous leap.[15]

The presence of a Jewish people beside the Christian Church
is a reminder to Christians that divine grace is not co-terminous
with their Church.

The word "Church", fifthly, is used in a still wider sense in
the conciliar documents. The Vatican Council gives an answer
to the crucial question of whether God has been redemptively at
work among men from the beginning.[16] Since we realize today
that mankind has existed for many long ages before the coming
of Christ, possibly half a million years, the question about human
history before Christ has assumed a new urgency. Are we to believe that God has hidden his love during these ages and left
man to his own resources, or may we, on the basis of the Gospel,
believe that God was redemptively engaged in the lives of men
from the very beginning? The Vatican Council unequivocally
replies that from the beginning, *inde ab initio,* God has surrounded the human family, caught in sin, with the means of
salvation. The love of God has always manifested itself in the
lives of men. God has always been saviour.

In this context the *Constitution on the Church* takes up an
ancient expression, found in patristic literature. The conciliar
text speaks of "the Church from Abel on".[17] Beginning with
Abel there was a community of men touched by divine grace and
open to the goodness offered them. "Church universal",[18] then,
may have a very wide meaning: Vatican II uses it to refer to
the entire family of men inasmuch as they are touched and

transformed by God's saving grace—the true dimension of which is revealed to us only in Jesus Christ. In a strictly doctrinal sense, therefore, we may call Church the community of men, extending as far as the human race, we are open to the Spirit and in whose hearts God creates good will.

How is this universal Church, this Church from Abel on, related to the Christian Church? The conciliar documents do not deal with this question in detail. It is suggested more than once, however, that the grace of God operative in the whole of humanity is dependent on Jesus Christ, the one mediator between God and man, and hence also related to the Church which is his body. From the beginning, the gift of grace producing holy community foreshadowed the Church of Christ. The action of God among people, initiating them into fellowship, prepared the full manifestation of his mercy in Christ and the community which is his body. The Vatican Council does not hesitate to make the double affirmation—however difficult this way may make it to present a perfectly coherent theology of God's self-revelation—that Church is the world-wide community of all men in which God creates faith and love and that Church is the Christian community in which alone Christ is proclaimed and celebrated.

The application of "Church universal" to the entire human race under the influence of divine grace, is of greatest doctrinal significance. We shall have to deal with this in greater detail further on. While this designation may appear startling when compared with the main emphasis of traditional teaching, it is less surprising when we relate it to the traditional position on the one divine finality of human life. If, in scholastic terminology, the one final end of the human race is supernatural then it follows—since the final cause is the cause of causes (*causa causarum*)—that the history of man and the dynamism of human life are supernatural. Designating the entire family of man as "Church universal" is equivalent to saying—in scholastic terminology—that human history is supernatural.

Finally, there is a sixth sense in which the word "Church" is significantly used. The *Constitution on the Church* speaks of God's redemptive action in the lives of men, especially in the unity of the family: in this connection it uses the expression "*ecclesia domestica*" or "house church".[19] The community of father, mother, children is here called Church. The meaning of this usage is clear. Since the members of the family are united among themselves through bonds created by faith, hope, and love, since, in other words, God is present to this community in the Spirit as the source of growth and human unfolding, it is possible to speak of it as Church. Church takes place when, through God's presence, the many are reconciled into one. Church happens when men come to love one another. Church is where people become friends.

This examination of the ways in which the word "Church" is used in the conciliar documents allows us to conclude that Vatican II freely and joyfully acknowledges a Spirit-created communion in Christ that transcends the visible boundaries of the Catholic Church. From a restrictive or closed understanding of Church, Catholic teaching at the Vatican Council has developed to an inclusivist understanding of Church. The Catholic Church is here presented as a community with open doors. The fellowship which Christ creates in the Church is not limited to the Church: it includes other Christians and their Churches. Even beyond the baptismal covenant the Spirit creates a redemptive bond or gracious solidarity between Christians and the rest of men. The Catholic Church has visible boundaries, but these are not barriers to communion and brotherhood. This we call the Open Church.

The open understanding of Church, we note, also affects the way in which we see the Catholic Church as a society. When, in the pre-conciliar period, we understood Church in exclusivist terms, we tended to restrict the term to the total social organization of the Catholic Church. We equated Church with Roman Catholic Church. As we were unwilling to call Church communities outside of this Roman Catholic Church, so we were unwilling to call Church communities within it. We overlooked the doctrinal understanding of local Churches and tended to see them simply as administrative divisions of the whole Catholic Church. The doctrinal development to an open understanding of Church, therefore, has immediate effects on the self-understanding of the Catholic Church as a human community. We have abandoned an administrative or juridical notion of unity! The Catholic Church is one because, through the inter-connectedness of its life, in faith, sacraments, and ministry, the one Church of Christ is present in the local Churches and in their union as a single people of God.

The doctrinal development at Vatican II has led to an inclusivist understanding of Church. We have seen that "Church" is the community of men known as Roman Catholics, "Church" is the local congregation of Christians, "Church" is the community of all the baptized, "Church" is an ecclesiastical community even when it is not in union with Rome, "Church" is the Abrahamic community, "Church" is the entire human race as redeemed by Christ, "Church", finally, is the fellowship of people who become friends. What, we must ask, is the doctrinal principle on which this use of the word Church is based? What is the theology behind this open view of the Church? The

27

conciliar documents do not deal with this question in detail. Theological synthesis is hardly the task of an ecclesiastical council. Yet the conciliar documents provide many hints that are useful to the Catholic theologian in this attempt to articulate a deeper understanding of the redemptive mystery revealed in Christ, that justifies the Open Church of Vatican II.

THE SIN OF THE WORLD

The Word of God reveals to us the ambiguity of human life.[20] Man is a sinner. Man is alienated from himself and from others. He bears within himself a division that taints every expression of his personality. There are, indeed, many possibilities for human existence, and with divine help man is able to grow, to become himself, to advance in holiness and the perception of truth, but however much progress in grace he makes, every manifestation of human life—apart from Jesus—retains an element of ambiguity. However much man grows in holiness he always remains in need of redemption. This need of redemption is a basic and unchangeable characteristic of life on earth.

Man is a prisoner of his own dividedness. He cannot extricate himself from this situation unless he is summoned from beyond himself. Left to himself, the forces of egotism and pride prevent him from growing as a human being; and in a world that is always moving, that is, in a world that is history, to cease growing means to enter into death.

This inevitably sinful situation in which a man is born and in which he cannot grow up without being profoundly marked by it, we call original sin. Man is born in original sin. Human life is such that a man cannot come into this world and grow up without being damaged by the sinfulness of his environment—mother, father, the family, the whole of society—and hence without becoming a sinner himself.

This understanding of original sin is suggested by Paul's presentation of sin in the Letter to the Romans. Let us look more closely at his teaching. In the first two chapters Paul describes the sinfulness that characterizes the whole of human existence. Man is a sinner and hence in need of redemption, whether he belongs to the nations of the world or to the chosen people of Israel. Paul dramatically describes the ignorance and hard-heartedness that characterised the civilization with which he was in contact. While God has summoned all men to come to true understanding, people have closed their hearts to him, they have become idolators, they have turned away from the truth and introduced disorder into their lives and chaos into society. St. Paul regarded the sexual confusion of his day as the symbol of the chaos that prevailed in the social life of men. But, Paul continues, the need for redemption is found not only among the nations; in Israel, too, men are sinners and in need of forgiveness and new life. While God has revealed his wisdom to the people of Israel, the generations have listened badly to his voice and refused to follow the divine summons with true dedication. Israel, too, is sinful.

What Paul is describing in the first two chapters of Romans is the sinfulness of the human race, a theme repeatedly taken up in the Old Testament, especially in the prophetic books and the psalms. Man is wretched. He is small, insignificant, destined to die. More than that, man tends to evil. To sin comes natural to him. This wretchedness of man is universal. It affects all men whatever their nation. This wretchedness is the human condition. Because of it, man and God are hardly compatible.

The New Testament—even apart from St. Paul—confirms the description of the human situation present in Old Testament literature. The Fourth Gospel speaks of "the sin of the world". This sin is to be deaf to God. This sin is to close one's ears to the divine voice, to be proud and selfish, and to hate those who listen to God's voice and do his will. This is the sin of the world into which men are born, and from which, according to the New Testament, Jesus saves them.

Paul approaches the sin of the world from a different viewpoint in chapter 5 of his Letter to the Romans.[21] There he speaks of the origin of this condition, and describes, on the basis of the biblical Adam-story, how sin has inserted itself into human history and how it has affected all men and passes on to them its dreadful effect which is death. Paul personalizes sin in this chapter. He speaks of sin as a tyrant who victoriously makes his way through human history and prepares the coming of another power, namely death. As Adam has sinned and then died—died in many ways, died especially to the true life—so all men since Adam have, in his image, been sinners and been taken over by death.

It is not easy to tell whether Paul regarded the story of Adam as a historical description of what happened in the past, or whether he followed a trend found in rabbinical literature where the story of Adam was used to say the significant things about human existence in general. In any case, there is good evidence that the chapter in Genesis from which the Adam-story is taken, was not meant to be history in the modern sense, as little, we may add, as the story of creation that precedes it.[22] There is good evidence for affirming that the opening chapters of Genesis—the stories of universal creation, the creation of man and his fall into sin—were not intended to be historical accounts of what happened a long time ago; they were intended to be the message of God to Israel revealing the meaning of human life. In the story of Adam and his fall—this is our only concern here—God made known to the people of Israel the situation in which they lived, in particular the sinfulness that pervaded human life—for which he, the Lord, was not responsible. The meaning of the Adam-story is manifold. But if it is true that this story was not intended to be an historical account, then we may not approach it with historical questions. We may not read the Adam-story as recorded in Genesis in the hope of finding replies to the questions, the many questions, we have about what happened at the beginning of human life: whether or not there was a sinless state in which man existed, whether or not the original man was of high intelligence and sensitivity, and so forth. To ask such questions of the Genesis narrative presupposes that this narrative was intended to supply information about what happened a long time ago, possibly at the beginning of human life on this earth. But the available evidence seems to point to the fact that the account was not written with this purpose in mind. If we have questions about what man was like at the beginning of human history, the only source of information available to us is scientific inquiry. The scriptures do not intend to give us information about the distant past.

The authors of the New Testament and the ecclesiastical writers ever since, have taught the inevitably sinful situation into which man is born and in which he, too, becomes sinner, by making use of the ancient Adam-story. We too may use this story. We may speak about the universal misery in which we live in terms of Adam and the fall of man, as long as we realize that we must use the story as it was meant in the Genesis narrative, that is, not as an historical account of what happened in

31

the past but as the divine message revealing the meaning of human life now.

In chapter 5 of Romans, we have said, St. Paul reveals the sinfulness of the human situation by speaking of "the sin that has entered the world". In chapter 7 of the same letter he deals with the sinful situation of man under a different image.[23] There he speaks about "the sin that dwells within". In other words, he describes the dividedness of man in psychological terms. He shows that man is not made of a piece; a part of him is inclined to do good and another part is inclined to do evil. These two tendencies are in conflict. By himself man is incapable of extricating himself from the prison of his dividedness. The conflicting inclinations in his heart prevent man from transcending his egotism and doing the will of God. "I can will what is right, but I cannot do it. For I do not do the good I want but the evil I do not want is what I do. Now if I do what I do not want, it is no longer I that do it, but sin which dwells within me."[24] It is only Christ, Paul declares, who enables men to leave the prison of human wretchedness. It is he alone who enables a man to leave his dividedness behind and become more truly a person dedicated to love and fidelity. The all-pervasiveness of sin is here told by a careful description of what happens in ordinary human life. A phenomenology of human action enables Paul to reveal the nature of the human predicament. Man is inevitably a sinner and hence in need of redemption.

There is evidence then for asserting that the three accounts of universal sin, presented in the Letter to the Romans, are actually dealing with one and the same reality. That reality, which the Church in later years has called "original sin," is presented in the first two chapters of Romans as "the sin of the world", in chapter 5 as "the sin that has entered the world," and in

chapter 7 as "the sin that dwells within". This justifies our definition of original sin as the inevitably sinful situation in which
a man is born and in which he cannot grow up without being
affected by it and becoming a sinner himself.

The expression "original sin" says that sin has existed among
us from the beginning. Man is born into it. Original sin is not
the result of man's free choice; he has inherited it. It is man's
inevitable heritage. At the same time God is not responsible for
it. Some Christians find great difficulty with such a concept.
How can something be called sin that has not been freely
chosen? How can a man become a sinner without freely con-
senting to it? How can there be a sin that is not strictly personal? In other words, how can sin be inherited?

It seems to me, however, that the traditional doctrine of
original sin gives an excellent account of how people experience
the human predicament and the dividedness of their hearts. As
we grow up we find ourselves divided. We discover the presence
of egotism in us. We are, in fact, quite unhappy about the self-
centredness and the pride which is part of us. As we live through
various situations we are quite amazed at the intensity of our
egotism. As we grow older and come to greater self-knowledge,
we find the dividedness of our hearts is much deeper than we
suspected. We seem to be caught in a predicament that prevents
us from living, that tends to make us incapable of loving, and
of being present to others and to the world. There is an element
of surprise in this self-discovery. Where does this egotism come
from? we ask ourselves. I did not choose it, we say to ourselves;
It is not really me, it is only part of me. A man is convinced
that he can distinguish himself from this power that makes him
self-centred and consequently deaf to reality. The evil in me is
not me. It seems to us, rather, that we have inherited it from

33

somewhere; we have picked it up somewhere without knowing it; we are sure that we have never chosen it; we feel it has become part of our life from forces extrinsic to ourselves.

At the same time a careful description of our dividedness also leads to the acknowledgement that the egocentricity that prevents me from love and openness to reality is my own, strictly my own. While I have not chosen it, I know that I am really endorsing it now. From one point of view my selfishness is a surprise to me and I insist that it has been passed on to me, but from another point of view this selfishness is really mine. It is I who love myself excessively. It is myself whom I put into the centre of my universe. My pride and egotism—infantile megalomania—may have invaded me from somewhere unknown to me, but now that I have discovered them in myself, I really know them to be mine, passionately mine. I realize that I cling to them and will not let them go. Even while I may hate the existence of this part in me, I endorse and re-endorse this part in me in a multitude of situations. My narcissism is really mine.

The doctrine of original sin, revealed in the New Testament and taught by the Church, makes known to us the predicament of the human situation and gives an account of it that corresponds to the double experience we have of our own dividedness; namely that we have inherited it and, at the same time, that it is profoundly our own. It is not mine, because I have not chosen it in the first place; it is very much mine, because I endorse it every day. The traditional teaching of the Church, it seems to me, is not a doctrine that poses great difficulties in the conceptual order. On the contrary, once we understand that this doctrine does not intend to present us with information about the remote past, the traditional teaching, based on the scriptural references, especially those of Paul in the Letter to the Romans, makes known to us the predicament which is ours and which, once articulated and acknowledged in faith, is not far removed from the experience we have of our dividedness.

Is this interpretation of original sin in harmony with the defined teaching of the Catholic Church? It seems to me that it is. As we mentioned before, the ecclesiastical councils express their teaching in terms taken from the Genesis narrative and hence do not intend to give more information about the past than this account does. Since it can be shown—the evidence for this, as we mentioned, is overwhelming—that this account had no intention of recording history, we must interpret the conciliar documents dealing with original sin in the same way. Whatever the fathers of a council may have personally believed about the first man, they had no intention of saying more about the universal sin in human life than is revealed in the scriptures.

Does the teaching of the Council of Trent that original sin is passed on "by generation"[25] present a difficulty to the doctrinal understanding here proposed? The answer is negative.[26] If we understand the word "generation" in a purely biological way, then the Council of Trent would teach that the sin dwelling within us is handed on by parents in the biological process of bringing children into the world; and this would rule out the interpretation presented in these pages. It seems more reasonable, however, to understand the word "generation" not in a biological, but in a fully human way. A man is generated by mother and father not simply by biological procreation; in the process of becoming a human person, a man receives more from his mother and father than his biological existence. The love and care of the parents, the early education of the child, the entire family environment, these are factors that are essential to the generation of a human person. If "generation" is understood in this wider, more human way, then the Council of Trent asserts that original sin is handed on from parents to their children in a complex process—of which biological growth is only a part—by which children are made ready for human life, and then this teaching is in accord with the interpretation of original sin given above. For we have insisted that man is born into an inevitably sinful environment and that he cannot grow up and assume responsibility—this is "generation"—without having been seriously affected by sin and having become a sinner himself.

This, then, is the universal human predicament: the dividedness of man. Man is estranged from himself and from others.

THE REDEMPTIVE MYSTERY

This human predicament is only half the story about man. There is another power at work in human life. Wherever people come together, something happens to them. They are summoned to pass beyond themselves and freed to leave their isolation and become friends. In and behind the misery which characterizes human existence is a mystery of new life that addresses man in his situation: that evokes new responses in him and enables him to leave his dividedness and become more truly himself. This mystery of new life which is present to human existence, is not of man's making. How could man, the prisoner, deliver himself? This mystery of new life which is at work wherever people are, is divine grace. God gives himself to men so that they may escape their isolation and become truly themselves.

The universality of God's redemptive action among men is clearly taught in the documents of Vatican II. This has been brought out in our remarks on the designations of the word

"Church". Church, we saw, is not only the Christian community; Church is also the whole of mankind as transformed by grace and the fellowship of people who become friends. I have presented a more detailed analysis of the conciliar teaching on the universality of divine grace in another volume.[27] In the present context, I simply refer to an explicit and formal declaration in the *Pastoral Constitution on the Church in the Modern World*. In a chapter presenting the paschal mystery of Christ as source and pattern of all Christian life, we are told that the same is true of human life everywhere. "Since Christ died for all men and since the ultimate vocation of man is, in fact, one and divine, we must hold that the Holy Spirit, in a manner known only to God, offers to every man the possibility of being associated with this paschal mystery."[28]

God's redemptive involvement in human history is repeatedly alluded to in the scriptures, even if it is not always at the centre of the biblical message. Central in the Bible is the special history of salvation. Central is the history of Israel in which God made himself known in preparation for the universal and final manifestation in Jesus Christ. Central is Jesus Christ in whom the grace of God is fully revealed. In Christ God has made himself visible. In him God comes to men in an unconditional and definitive way. But the centrality of this special history of salvation does not prevent the scriptures from dealing with the wider history of salvation, embracing the whole of mankind, the reality and meaning of which is revealed in the person of Christ.

There are several universalist themes in the Old Testament. They are not central, they may be overlooked, but they are expressed with great clarity. Perhaps the most celebrated one is the story of the covenant named after Noah, which God makes with all the peoples of the earth.[29] We read in the book of

Genesis that after the flood and the destruction of all flesh, God establishes a covenant with Noah and through him with the entire human family. God promises that he will always protect human life on earth and never again permit the forces of nature to destroy it. To symbolize this covenant God puts the rainbow in the sky. This rainbow now commemorates the covenant of mercy which God has made between himself and the human race. Every time God sees the rainbow he will remember the everlasting covenant which he has made with the people of the earth.

It is highly likely that this story was told among the people of Israel as a reply to their questions about God's relationship to other nations. Israel had experienced the presence of God. He was their saviour. He had made them a people. He had revealed himself to them in a covenant of mercy, which summoned them to fidelity and obedience. But how was this God, who had revealed his condescension to Israel, related to other peoples? The story of the Noachic covenant replies to this.

While the literary source of the story and the exact meaning of its details may be unclear, the principal message is evident. God is merciful wherever people are. The relationship of God to the whole human race is designated by the word "covenant" that expresses Israel's existence as God's people. Covenant, everlasting covenant, expresses the presence of God to the whole human race. Beyond the errors, the blindness, and the confusion of men, there is a mystery of new life at work among them which discloses itself as the presence of the living God.

Another celebrated expression of the universalist theme is the Book of Jonah. This beautiful story was written at a time when an exclusivist understanding of the covenant was strong among the people of Jerusalem, especially the priesthood. Again and again Israel was tempted to regard its own election as a declaration of divine favour that restricted God's love to themselves. The prophets, especially the Second Isaiah, had insisted that the mercy of God and his plan of salvation went far beyond the boundaries of Israel. The book of Jonah, in a new situation, reminds the people of Israel that God loves the entire family of men and that Israel and its prophets have been elected as instruments of a salvation that extends to the ends of the earth. The book tells a story in which the city of Nineveh, the capital of Assyria, the archenemy of Israel, is gifted by God with repentance and receives forgiveness and new life. The story reports that Jonah, the prophet of Israel, is unhappy about the mercy shown to the Ninevites. He attempts to resist God. Through a series of imaginative incidents God pursues the prophet to open his mind to the marvellous reality of a mercy that is universal.

Another Old Testament theme revealing the presence of God to human life everywhere, is the understanding of creation found in the prophets.[30] In the prophetic literature divine creation does not usually refer to a divine action that took place in the past, at the beginning of time, when the universe began to exist; creation rather signifies the on-going divine action in the present by which things come to be and follow their course and, more important still, by which men come to be and enter into their history. Creation refers to the involvement of God in present life.[31] For this reason the prophetic literature does not always distinguish between creation and redemption. God's creation is his present action among men, which is always new, surprising, discriminating, and merciful, and hence rules the history of men and nations in view of universal redemption. God's ever-present creation is not simply his conserving action keeping his creatures in being and enabling them to follow the laws of their natures—

this is the way the scholastics may have thought of present creation—no, the ever-present creation of God is always new creation
and thus the redemption of his people. The prophetical teaching
of creation, then, announces the redemptive involvement of God
in the whole of human life.

Is God's redemptive involvement in the lives of men also
insinuated in the New Testament? The central message of the
Gospel is the person of Jesus Christ. Salvation is described, above
all, as man's encounter with Jesus Christ in faith and his participation in the life and worship of the Christian community.
Christ is the one mediator between God and man. Apart from
him there is no salvation. Yet even the New Testament does not
interpret this message in an exclusivist sense. The unique medita-
tion of Christ did not stop the apostles from acknowledging
God's redemptive work in Israel. Calling Christ the one mediator
between God and man did not prevent the apostolic Church
from teaching that in Israel men were saved by faith in the God
of the covenant, and that the call of Abraham and his response
to it in faith made him the father of all the faithful. The unique
mediation of Christ, therefore, was never understood in a narrow
literalistic sense. The grace of God present in Israel was related
to Christ as a way of preparation. Even before the coming of
Jesus then, God was at work in his Word, his Logos, summoning men to salvation and evoking in them the response of faith
and love.

In the Fourth Gospel we find the roots of a Logos theology
that was worked out in the Church of later centuries and that
enabled the Christians of antiquity to acknowledge the redemptive action of God in the entire history of mankind.[32] In the
Prologue of St. John we are told that the Word, the Logos, has
existed from the beginning with God and, in fact, that this

Word was God. Whether we understand Logos in reliance on the Old Testament concept of divine Word or Summons or in reliance on the Greek notion of intelligibility or meaning, the Prologue proclaims that from the beginning God was involved in the lives of men. From the beginning, and not only from the time of Jesus, God has been Summons or Meaning addressing men. The Word, we are told, is the light of men. It is source of life to them. The Prologue suggests this wide application and Christian tradition has confirmed it.

There are other universalist themes in the New Testament. The special history of salvation made known in Jesus Christ and usually proclaimed in highly restrictive terms, did not exclude a wider understanding of salvation history as embracing all mankind. The special history reveals the meaning of the universal history. In Jesus Christ, God makes known his involvement with people everywhere.

We find a universalist theme in Paul's letters to the Ephesians and Colossians. Jesus Christ is here proclaimed as the head of the Church and, beyond this, the head of the entire human race. Jesus is "the first-born of all creation." Why? Because in him, in his image, all things and especially all people have been created and are still being created. Christ is before all things and in Christ all things hold together. The mystery of redemption, present in a hidden way from the beginning, is fully revealed in the historical Christ, in whom God has overcome the hostility between man and man and reconciled the human race as a single family.

In his Letter to the Ephesians St. Paul presents Jesus Christ as the head of the human race in a twofold order: in accordance with what happened from the beginning of human life and in accordance with what happened through his death and resurrection.[33] The apostle does not clarify how these two aspects are connected. But he suggests that the mystery, hidden from the beginning, is made known to men in the victory of Christ. Again it is insinuated, without being explicitly affirmed, that the redemptive action of God, which is manifest in Christ's work of salvation, has been operative from the beginning among people, however obscure this action may have been and however great man's opposition to it.

There is, moreover, some evidence for regarding as a universalist theme the opposition between the first Adam and Jesus, the second Adam, in the Letter to the Romans, chapter 5.[34] Adam, the sinner, is a key for the understanding of human life. Man is divided. He is a prisoner of his own self-centredness. He grows up in this world, in the likeness of Adam, a sinner. The sin and its consequences, described in the Adam-story, reveal the situation into which each man is born. Yet the Good News is that Adam is not the only key to the understanding of human life. The true key to the understanding of man is Jesus Christ, the second Adam. It is possible to look at man only in terms of the powers of self-destruction, alive in him. It is possible to see in man only his sin. Our experience may incline us to regard men and perhaps especially ourselves in this dark light. Simply left to ourselves we are hopelessly lost. Yet the Good News proclaimed by Paul is that Adam is not the full key to the understanding of human life. The true reality of human life is revealed only in Christ. There is in man not only the inner estrangement, there is also a transcending power at work in him, in and behind his misery, a mystery of grace which summons him into becoming more fully human and enables him to trust, to hope and to love. Christ is alive in man. Christ dwells by faith in the hearts of men. A man is not delivered over to the forces of self-destruction, he is not condemned to remain a prisoner of his own self-centredness. This is what we might think if Adam were the first-born or the type of every man. The Good News, however, proclaims that Christ is the first-born or the type of every man. God has involved himself in the life of every man to lead him to perfect manhood, the ultimate dimension of which is only revealed in Jesus Christ. While the forces of sin are strong, we are told by Paul that the forces of new life are even stronger. The mystery of salvation, at work wherever people are, summons men to leave the isolation created by their sin and to enter into friendship and be open to the ever-present guidance of the Spirit.

The biblical themes of Old and New Testaments which we have discussed are not central in the biblical literature. Yet at various times in her history and more especially in our own day, the Church has focused on these themes and formulated her teaching in reliance on them. This happened, as we saw, at the Vatican Council. In a later chapter we shall examine how this doctrinal development has taken place.

We realize that the doctrine of God's redemptive involvement in human life raises many theological problems. Some of them arise from the biblical record, others from the doctrine of the Church. How can this teaching be reconciled with the unique mediation of Christ, with the saving mission of the Church, with the necessity of baptism, with justification by faith, and with the presence of evil? We cannot go into these problems in this chapter. Some of the issues raised will become clearer in the course of this study.

Christian wisdom has always acknowledged that we cannot understand man simply by looking at man. Pascal said, man is always more than man. A mystery of new life is at work among people, captive as they are in their sinfulness. The true dimension of this mystery is revealed to us only in Jesus Christ. Human life is never reducible to man alone. To have a true understanding of human life we must take account of a reality that transcends man. This "more than man" in human life is the redemptive mystery in which God reveals himself.

This teaching has been formulated in many ways. In traditional theological language we might simply say that human life is always supernatural.[35] God is redemptively involved in the life of every single person. Man may indeed resist the divine summons and be insensitive to his gifts—this is true in the Church as well as outside—but the Good News assures us that God never leaves men without the means of salvation. In his concrete situation man is again and again summoned by God to leave his dividedness behind and enter more deeply into the unity of truth and love. In every situation of life, in manner altogether gratuitous and surprising, God offers men the freedom to become more truly themselves. God has involved himself, in the Spirit, in the personal and social dynamics by which men become more conformed to the likeness of Jesus, the perfect man.

The mystery of redemption, then, is part of human history. It is an entirely gratuitous and marvellous way and yet it is properly co-constitutive of human history, personal and social. This mystery of new life can be described in a variety of ways. Since we have regarded sin, above all, as dividedness, we wish to present the mystery of redemption, operative in the human family, as a divine work of reconciliation—or as the ecclesial mystery.

Man is born into dividedness. His self-centredness makes him incapable of love. He cannot go out of himself and be friends with others. Sin is isolation. Yet the mystery of new life, present

44

wherever people are, appeals to man in his situation. Through others who are close to him a man is summoned, is loved, is made free to respond, and as he replies to a new call, he dies a little to his selfishness and rises to a new dimension of love. Through others he comes to know who he is; through others he is made capable of love; through others he finds himself as a member of a community.

This process of human growth through the summons and gifts of others is evident in childhood. The infant would not achieve consciousness unless a mother called him by his name, surrounded him with care, and offered her love as the foundation of his own responses to her. A child receives everything from the family in which he lives—his language, his reasoning, his emotional life. We become ourselves through others. This is true for the child but this is also true for the adult. We need others to become ourselves.

A phenomenological analysis of dialogue and participation would show that a man is enabled to leave his dividedness and move into self-possession through his association with others. Love on an interpersonal level and involvement in the wider community in terms of truth and action, deliver a man from connatural self-centredness and initiate him into his humanity. A man's response to the summons and his acceptance of the gifts offered him by others—who themselves are challenged by him—is an essential factor in the on-going creation of his person.

Christians believe that the summons and the gifts which are offered to men in the process of becoming themselves are, in the last analysis, from God—they are God's presence to man. For God is Word. It is God who summons man and by summoning him constitutes him as a person. God is Gift. It is God who comes to man enabling him to respond to the summons and thus to become more truly himself. We believe that the God who has revealed himself in Christ has involved himself in the humanization of man. He has involved himself in human history as Word and as Spirit, as Word addressing man and as Spirit freeing man to respond in love. Christians believe, moreover, that this redemptive presence of God to man takes place, always and everywhere, through other men. God comes to us through the mediation of history. He comes to us in human life. The mode of divine self-communication is incarnation. Whether in ordinary human life through conversation and interaction or, more specifically, in the Church through message and sacrament, God always comes through the mediation of men. God is present to people in the process of becoming more truly themselves, not by intervening in their lives from a point outside of history but by summoning and gracing them from within the human situation in which they live.

The Christian believes that it is God's presence to human life that enables men to become friends. A mystery is at work wherever people come together. As they engage in conversation and seek to solve the problems of life together something happens which we acknowledge as divine grace or a mystery of reconciliation. Since man is born into original sin and thus is a prisoner of his own dividedness, we realize that the presence of love and selflessness in his life is due to the free and unmerited grace of God. Wherever people gather God offers to them— through one another—the grace of fellowship. Men may resist the summons and close themselves to the love offered them, but because of God's revelation in Christ we believe that wherever people talk to one another and join in solving the problems of life, the mystery of redemption offers them fellowship on different levels and in different ways and thus empowers them to become more truly themselves and enter into salvation.

Divine grace creates fellowship. For this reason theologians have said that wherever grace is given to men, from the very beginning of history, it has an ecclesial character. Grace is always ecclesial. The presence of God in the lives of men makes them friends. If we abstract from this mystery, a gathering of men would simply be a group of insular beings, each separated from the other by the dividedness of his own existence. Abstracting from this mystery, the gathering of men would be immersed in ambiguity: it would result in the playing of games, possibly sinister games, each man trying to use the other, and at the same time falling into the trap of his own helplessness. Yet God's gift of himself is never totally absent from people. His self-communication offers and creates community. This is the mystery of Church.

We have now come to an understanding of the mystery of Church that enables us to account for the manifold way in which the word "Church" is used in the documents of Vatican II. We may speak of Church whenever and wherever people become friends through God's presence to them. The ecclesial mystery manifests itself in many different ways, in different intensities and modalities, in varying degrees of partiality and completeness. The mystery of Church becomes already visible where two people become friends and by doing so open themselves to salvation. We may call Church, with the documents of Vatican II, the totality of men in whom God creates faith and love as well as the few who, through God's presence have become brothers. Yet since it is only in Christ that the mystery of redemption, at work in human history, is made known to man and spelled out in his life, death, and resurrection, we call Church in a specific sense only the Christian community. Church is the fellowship created by God's self-communication through Christ in the power of the Spirit. In the Church of Christ this divine self-communication takes place in a special way through the gifts which Christ gave his followers: the Gospel and the sacramental liturgy. In Word and sacrament the Father comes in a special way to his people —is present to them through Christ in the Spirit and thus constitutes them as the Church fully manifest in human history. Church is, therefore, Christian Church. Since as Catholics we believe that the gifts of Christ are present in the Catholic Church in keeping with his own self-revelation, Church is for us especially Catholic Church.

THE CHURCH AND THE CHURCHES

The doctrine of the Church, as we have seen, tells us something about men and human society everywhere. By the word "Church" we express our faith in a mystery of redemption that is operative wherever people are. Church signifies for us a worldwide Spirit-created communion among men. At the same time, this universal understanding of Church does not devaluate the specific character and role of the Christian Church. The universality of grace does not obliterate the distinction between Church and humanity.

The Christian Church is the community in which Jesus Christ, in whom God reveals himself unconditionally and definitively, is proclaimed and celebrated. It is the community in which the mystery of salvation, present everywhere in a hidden manner but spelled out in detail in the crucified and risen Lord, is professed and believed. It is the community in which Christ is present through his gifts historically delivered to the apostles. The Christian Church is the visible sign and the perpetual pledge of that mystery which works in the whole of human history and leads men into truth and friendship. Seen in this perspective the Christian Church remains open to communion with men beyond her boundaries since the mystery of salvation, which Christians consciously acknowledge and publicly profess, is at work in the entire human family.

This understanding of the ecclesial mystery, moreover, enables us to affirm the presence of Christ's Church in all the Christian Churches and, in a unique way, in the Catholic Church.

We must recall at this point the doctrinal development at Vatican II that enabled the Catholic Church to acknowledge the ecclesial reality of other Christian Churches. The preconciliar ecclesiology, expressed in authoritative ecclesiastical documents, presented the Catholic Church as the true Church of Christ in such an exclusive way that it was unable to acknowledge that other Churches were also Churches in a doctrinal sense. This has changed at the Vatican Council.[36]

In one of the earlier drafts of the *Constitution of the Church* a sentence identified, in an unqualified manner, the Church of Christ and the Catholic Church. This had been the teaching of pre-conciliar ecclesiology, strongly supported by Pope Pius XII. Yet the discussion on the Council floor revealed that many bishops wished to modify the strict identity between Church of Christ and Catholic Church in order to leave room for a positive doctrinal evaluation of other Christians and other Christian Churches. In keeping with these demands the sentence was modified, and instead of saying that the Church of Christ "is" the Catholic Church, the final text declares that this Church "subsists in" the Catholic Church.[37] The meaning of the word "subsists" is not explained; the notes accompanying the text simply indicate that the word was inserted in order to indicate the presence of ecclesial elements outside the Catholic Church.

Another significant change in the self-understanding of the Catholic Church is recorded in the *Decree on Ecumenism*. Here the ecclesial reality of other Churches is clearly acknowledged.[38] While the decree reaffirms the uniqueness of the Catholic Church as the all-embracing means of salvation (*generale auxilium salutis*), it also teaches that other Christian Churches are used by the Spirit to save and sanctify men and, consequently, that they belong to the ecclesial mystery of salvation. According to the decree, Christ is present in the Christian Churches through his gifts of faith, hope, and charity, as well as through the visible elements of Christian worship, including the Gospel message. The reference to the visible elements by which Christ is present in the Christian community enables the decree to affirm the uniqueness of the Catholic Church and, at the same time, acknowledge the ecclesial reality of other Christian Churches.

According to Vatican II, it is "through the Catholic Church alone—the all-embracing means of salvation—that the fullness of the means of salvation can be obtained".[39] Or again, "It was to the apostolic college alone, of which Peter is the head, that we believe that our Lord entrusted all the blessings of the New Covenant, in order to establish on earth the one Body of Christ into which all those should be fully incorporated who belong in any way to the people of God".[40] The understanding seems to be that the Catholic Church as institution is created through the celebration of the gifts of Christ—doctrinal, sacramental and ministerial—in their adequate form. Other Christian Churches exist as institutions through the celebration of some of these gifts. While the Catholic Church believes that the other

Churches are in some way defective in institutional terms, she acknowledges that Christ is present to them and is willing and happy to call them Churches.

This doctrinal evaluation of what Christian Churches are, enables us to give a more precise meaning to the phrase "subsists in", employed in the *Constitution on the Church*. The mystery of Church is manifested in the history of men in a variety of ways. It was present from the beginning wherever people became friends through the presence of God to them. It appeared visibly in the people of Israel when God was present to his people in virtue of his public revelation and in terms of the ancient covenant of his mercy. Through Christ, in the power of the Spirit, the Church was made manifest in its final form. The Church of Christ is formally constituted as community by the mystery of reconciliation present to the whole of life. The Church of Christ is historically present in the Catholic Church in the adequate way. It is present institutionally through the completeness of the gifts Christ bestowed on his people. This is what is meant by saying that the Church of Christ "subsists in" the Catholic Church. But the same Church of Christ is historically present also in the other Christian Churches, even if this happens in forms that Catholics believe to be, in various ways, less than adequate. The same Church of Christ which subsists in the Catholic Church in the adequate way, also subsists in the other Christian Churches in variously less than adequate forms.

It seems undeniable that at Vatican II the Catholic Church still makes an exclusive claim for herself. The conciliar documents do not explain in concrete terms what this uniqueness means. It certainly does not mean that salvation and holiness are less available in the other Christian Church. Since redemptive communion is created by the Spirit and hence is only condi-

51

tionally dependent on institutional elements, it is clear that the institutional adequacy which is claimed for the Catholic Church in no way implies that the Catholic Church as a Christian community is more transformed into God's people than any other Christian Church. It would be presumptuous to suggest, for instance, that the institutional adequacy of a Catholic diocese or parish guarantees a more intense presence of the ecclesial mystery in it than in a corresponding congregation of another Church, Orthodox, Protestant, or Anglican. The presence of the Spirit in a Church is related to the ecclesiastical institution only conditionally. What, then, is the uniqueness which the Catholic Church still claims for herself at Vatican II? It must be something that belongs to the institutional order.

The special claim of the Catholic Church has become embarrassing to many Catholics today. Is this claim a last remnant of ecclesiastical pride, or is it fidelity to a divine promise? We shall have to examine this question in chapter 4.

New and startling at the Vatican Council was the acknowledgement of the other Christian Churches as Churches. This doctrinal development created the foundation for the Catholic participation in the ecumenical movement. On this new basis the movement for Christian unity cannot possibly consist in persuading Christians to leave one Church in order to join another or in working for the conversion of any one Church to principles that are alien to her. What ecumenism means, for Catholics and other Christians, in a movement of dialogue and cooperation between the Churches seeking greater fidelity to Christ and enlarging the common ground between them. This movement is destined to transform the self-understanding of the Churches until the differences that separate them no longer justify the existing division. Then—if this should be the course

of history—the unity of Christians will become possible in an ecclesiastical union in which each Church remains faithful to what
it regards as its own divine charge or heritage.

Vatican II has defined the ecumenical movement in the same
terms as the World Council of Churches. This, at least, is my
understanding of the matter. There is a single ecumenical movement in which each Church participates according to principles
in keeping with its own self-understanding. As the movement
develops these principles change. Why? Because dialogue and
common action modify the self-understanding of the Churches
involved and thus enlarge the basis on which they may participate in the movement.

In recent years, however, this understanding of ecumenism
has been challenged by many Christians. As we shall see further
on, some Christians regard the ecumenical movement as too
narrowly conceived. What is wrong with ecumenism, they say,
is that it is confined to Christians. Since God is redemptively
at work in the whole of humanity, the Church may well be in
need of dialogue and cooperation with all men in order to submit to God's Word in total obedience. We may find that the
Church needs the world to become Church. The doctrinal considerations of this chapter, according to which God is redemptively present to the whole world, will have a profound influence
on widening the understanding of ecumenism.

The doctrine of God's redemptive involvement in human life
leaves many questions open. What is the meaning of baptism?
If human life is the primary means of salvation, what is the
specific role of the sacraments? What is the difference between
Church and world? What is the Church's mission? These are
important questions. Since we want to move to the apologetical
issues raised by Charles Davis we cannot deal with them here.

I may assure the reader that these questions can be answered and, in fact, have been answered in contemporary theology. Karl Rahner and Edward Schillebeeckx have conclusively shown that the affirmation of God's redemptive presence in human history may demand that we re-interpret the meaning of baptism, of sacraments, of Church and her mission, but that this re-interpretation does not weaken the role of these divine gifts in the lives of men.[41]

We conclude from this chapter that at Vatican II the Catholic Church has acquired a new self-understanding. Through a startling doctrinal development we have passed from a restrictive to an inclusive understanding of Church. This doctrinal shift to the Open Church affects our evaluation of human life everywhere and of the ecumenical movement in particular. Church has become a divine message revealing what happens wherever people live in community.

2.

The Sick Society and the Spirit

ACCORDING to Charles Davis it no longer makes sense to be a Catholic. For him the claim to uniqueness which the Catholic Church at Vatican II still makes for herself has lost all meaning. The Church, he says, has become incredible. In *A Question of Conscience* Charles Davis tries to put down in systematic fashion the reasons why, according to him, the Catholic Church can no longer credibly present herself as the Church of Christ.

The Church, the sacramental presence of Christ in the world, must be a visible expression of faith, hope, and love. In a detailed analysis Charles Davis tries to show that the Catholic Church as institution is not a sign of faith, hope, and love, that it is, in fact, a counter-sign sending the message "the Church is not here." The Catholic reader of Charles Davis' book may feel that the description of the Church's sins is not very original. He has heard all this before. At present Catholic literature and the Catholic press carefully examine the faults of the institutional Church and bring to light the inadequacies of the system which, in the past, remained hidden behind what was regarded as loyal silence. It has become customary among Catholics to criticize the institutional Church, beginning with the pontifex maximus down to the last monsignor at the chancery, in the light of the Gospel and its mission in the world. The Catholic, nourished by this self-critical literature, will have a great deal of sympathy with the complaints of Charles Davis. He has heard them before, he has uttered many of them himself, he hears them repeated in endless variations at clerical gatherings and at parties where people reveal what they really think. All Catholics suffer from the ills of the system; the more they love the Church the more they are tormented by the teachings, the action, and the policies of the institutional Church which obscure faith, hope, and love.

The conclusion Charles Davis draws from the description seems extreme. Was the Church ever different? Were there not always counter-signs in the Church committed to proclaiming the Good News? Yet we shall take Charles Davis' presentation of ecclesiastical vice seriously and make it the starting point for our own theological reflections.

The Analysis of the Church's Ills

To show that the Catholic Church is a counter-sign of faith Charles Davis introduces two concepts, "the corruption of language" and "the zone of truth".[1] Human words can be corrupted. Instead of being used as vehicles of truth they can be employed as means of manipulating people with disregard to truth. Words can be used to hide reality. In an institution language can become a tool or weapon by which the institution asserts and defends itself, by which it promotes the *status quo,* and manipulates its members to suit its own ends. A zone of truth, in the vocabulary adopted by Davis, is a community where language is a vehicle of truth. A zone of truth is a dedicated community in which men struggle to use words well and refuse to use language as a means of manipulation. A zone of truth differs from a power structure that is preoccupied with its own position and prestige. A zone of truth is a community in which men become sensitive to truth, in which truth becomes strong, in which men commit themselves to truth even if it accuses them.

Charles Davis writes, "Now, to be a zone of truth is, as I see it, essential to the Church of Christ, because of the nature of Christian faith which presupposes an ultimate commitment to all truth. If a social body has ceased to be a zone of truth, it is no longer credible as the Church of Christ".[2]

Then he proceeds to show that the Catholic Church as institution is not a zone of truth. He goes through the many painful realities which a Catholic, especially a Catholic involved in ecclesiastical life, knows so well. He analyses the ambiguity and insincerity of ecclesiastical language, the secrecy, the desire to hide the truth, the concern with prestige, the willingness to use power to suppress truth, and so forth.

Does the ecclesiastical institution rejoice in truth? Or is it afraid of it? Does it welcome new insights? Does it encourage research? The history of the Church, even into our own day, records many instances revealing that the ecclesiastical institution is more interested in power and prestige than in the truth of things. New truth is always embarrassing. New truth unsettles and may demand a rethinking of traditional concepts and a restructuring of the social order.

Who would deny that the phenomena described by Davis exist in the Church? We know how frightened the ecclesiastical hierarchy can be of new questions and new answers. In the defense of what is regarded as traditional, the magisterium is sometimes less than frank. The concern for prestige only too often overrules the openness to truth. Since we have created an image of a sinless and unfailing Church, those in charge of the institution are often feverishly at work to keep this image intact. Language is thus used to preserve the image of the Church—or the papacy.

In this context the birth control issue, which deeply moved Charles Davis, is highly significant. We have mentioned it in the Introduction. A Catholic philosopher has recently described the Church's hesitation in regard to truth and her concern over prestige in a satirical observation. The Church, he remarked, reacts in regard to new truth first by saying "It is wrong", then, after some years, by admitting "It may not be wrong, but it is dangerous", and finally by claiming "The Church has taught it all the time . . ."

Charles Davis realizes that fear of truth and the building of the image are not the only forces at work in the Church. He acknowledges the ardent love of truth of many Christians in high and low positions in the Church and their readiness to oppose the corruption of language. But he does not find "their presence sufficient to save the credibility of the social structure".[3] He concludes, "I reached the conviction that the Roman Church is not a zone of truth but rather of untruth, and so is no longer credible for me as the embodiment of Christian faith".[4]

What about the Church and hope? Here too, Charles Davis thinks, it can be demonstrated that the Catholic Church is a counter-sign of hope.[5] Hope, according to the beautiful definition of Davis, is "the trusting assurance that the life in Christ which we now possess will prevail over every contrary force, including death itself".[6] This trusting assurance liberates from fear. The future is not a threat to us because we trust that even the adverse forces we shall encounter will not destroy us. The man of hope is open to the newness that appears in human life and history. He regards the present as provisional. He is not overly attached to the forms of life he has inherited and now cherishes; he wants to remain open to the newness that he encounters in the future. The Christian, therefore, while taking the institutions of this world seriously, retains a strong sense of the provisional. If, Charles Davis reasons, freedom from fear and a sense of the provisional are a sign of hope, then he can show that the Catholic Church as an institutional reality is not such a sign in the world. He finds it easy to point to a long historical period in which the Catholic Church was afraid of the world and resisted the advance of science and the development of society. For centuries the Church was a conservative political force in European history. Many of her policies in regard to cultural development and political evolution were dictated by fear. The ecclesiastical documents of the 19th century provide Charles Davis with ample material to demonstrate this. The historical record, reaching into the present, shows that the Catholic Church is strongly attached to her own past, to the existing order, to her own self-image— in other words that she is lacking a sense of the provisional. Until this day, Charles Davis thinks, the policies of the Catholic hierarchy have been largely based on the desire to protect and promote the system.

How does Charles Davis deal with the extraordinary evolution that has taken place in the Catholic Church at Vatican II? It seems to me that he underestimates the changes that have taken place. He attributes the new thought and the new policies in the Church to the slow assimilation of secular experience, scientific and political, of Western society and gives credit for the entry of these new ways in the Church only to theologians and lay people. "The structure of hierarchical authority has had little to do with the present renewal."[7] This, I think, is untrue. The Vatican Council was an institutional event.

What about the Church and love? Again Davis tries to show that the Catholic Church has ceased to be a sign of love in the world.[8] He insists that he is not opposed to institutions as such. Institutions are necessary to express social life and promote it. His point is that the institution of the Catholic Church is an antiquated structure, out of harmony with the thinking, the needs, and the aspirations of modern Christians conscious of their mission in the world. The institutional Church does not serve the growth of persons nor strengthen them in their commitment to truth. On the contrary, the Church has subordinated persons and truth to its own institutional ends. Christians survive in dignity and freedom in the Catholic Church only if they move to the outer limit and reduce their connection with the institution to a minimum. He concludes, "An archaic institution, because destructive in its effects, becomes a heretical structure".[9] The Catholic Church, then, in the eyes of Charles Davis has become a counter-sign of the Gospel.

To illustrate his thesis that the Catholic Church has subordinated persons to the institutions Charles Davis turns to the present crisis in religious life and the priesthood. He shows that the structures of religious congregations, especially of women, are antiquated, that they reflect a cultural expression of an age gone by, and that men and women who look at life as modern Christians often find it impossible to serve the Gospel and grow as human beings in these institutions. Davis points to similar inadequacies in the institutional priesthood.

As an example of another inadequacy of the Church as institution we might point to the simple fact that there are no courts in the Church in which a Christian may seek the defense of his rights when they are threatened. In the present system legislator and judge are the same person. The inadequacy of this present system is lamented by a growing number of Catholics.

A shocking example illustrating the impersonal and often heartless character of the institution and the lack of protection available to persons is reported in an article in *The Commonweal*[10] published after the appearance of *A Question of Conscience*. It dealt with the manner in which priests seeking dispensation from the ministry are treated by the establishment. They receive contradictory information about procedures, they are encouraged to denigrate their own character, they are humiliated by compromising questionnaires, they are left without a reply for a long time—sometimes for many years. No clear regulations regarding the granting of dispensations have been made public. These priests—and there are hundreds of them—depend on the whims of individuals in authority. A few priests have received dispensations. Sometimes, if their intention is to get married, they are advised by the chancery office to get married in the city hall and then come back to have their marriage secretly acknowledged by the Church. No wonder that priests decide to take their future into their own hands.

These shortcomings and abuses of the ecclesiastical institution and the antiquated character of many Church structures are today freely expressed and analyzed by Catholics. How, then, can Charles Davis use this critique of the institution as an argument against the Catholic Church? This critique is, after all, a product of the Catholic Church. He follows his general tendency here. He interprets the renewal in the Church as a fringe phenomenon. He writes, "Particularly in Holland and America,

61

there is an upsurge of thinking and writing that cannot be reconciled with the doctrinal stance of the Roman Church, nor assimilated, I think, into its present structure. And that, I might add, is also the judgment of Pope Paul and most bishops".[11] Charles Davis interprets the present struggles of reform and renewal in the Catholic Church, not as authentic expressions of the Church but, rather, as so many indications that the institutional Church is falling apart and that a radically new pattern of Christian life, beyond confessional boundaries, is emerging. This thesis, as we shall see, he develops at length in the latter part of his book. Davis regards the present renewal in the Church as a movement extrinsic to her life so that it does not affect the sign-character of the Church in the world.[12] This, I think, is an incorrect historical evaluation of contemporary Catholic life.

We have reviewed the argument of Charles Davis in some detail. Catholics admit—with sadness and, often, with anguish—that most of what he says about us is correct. It seems to me, however, and I have indicated this in the preceding pages, that the sweeping character of his descriptions makes him insensitive to the Spirit-created realities in the Church that would modify his generalizations and thus lead him to more modest conclusions.

At the same time, Charles Davis' analysis of what faith, hope, and love mean for the Church is interesting and instructive. In a more traditional ecclesiology, we understood the faith of the Church in reference to the content of divine revelation, her hope in reference to the glory that is promised, and her love in reference to the holiness of her members. But the moral sensitivity of man changes. To follow Christ today means something that, from many points of view, it did not mean in the past. I regard it as a significant contribution to Catholic ecclesiology to understand the Church's faith, hope, and love in terms of the commitment to be a zone of truth, redeeming language from corruption, to be open to the future and possess a sense of the provisional, and to give institutional expression to the lives of people and serve them in their growth as men and as community.

I wish to reflect more systematically on the ills of the Church described by Charles Davis. I do not think that they are random manifestations of human sin. They are not simply due to the fact that the men in charge of the institution are lacking in personal holiness. It would be an injustice to attribute the present ills of the institution to lack of virtue on the part of popes and bishops. It seems to me that the ills which Davis describes follow a pattern that can be analyzed. In fact, these faults of the Catholic Church present a phenomenon that is by no means peculiar to the Catholic Church: in different degrees they exist also in other institutions. My thesis is that Charles Davis has described in the Catholic Church the social pathology that threatens every institution.

Every society is capable of forms of behaviour that may be called pathological. Institutions created to express and serve the life of a community can be drawn into irrational behaviour by forces of which those responsible for institutions are hardly aware. An institution is always vulnerable: it can fail to serve the community for the sake of which it was created and regard itself as its own end. Societies are vulnerable to a kind of behaviour that is not so much determined by conscious choices than by hidden forces in the institution. It is, of course, possible that the malice of men in government be responsible for the destructive effects of the institution. There is, however, a kind of irrational behaviour of societies that is produced, not by conscious decisions, but by spontaneous and half-conscious reactions of men in charge of the institution. In other words, institutions are vulnerable to sickness. The ill effects of social organizations are not reducible to the malice of their members nor to the sins of the policy-makers; there are other forces connected with the role of the institution that are capable of drawing society into actions and policies that undermine the purpose for the sake of which it exists. I do not wish to suggest that these forces are totally independent from personal responsibility; they may indeed be affected by the men of the institution; but the power which people, even those in government, have over these forces is quite limited. The dynamics operative in institutions make certain forms of irrational behaviour a perpetual possibility. It is not that every institution is pathological; but every institution is vulnerable to pathological deformations. It seems to me that Charles Davis' description of the evils in the Catholic Church bring out certain forms of social behaviour that have a much wider application.

SOCIAL PATHOLOGY IN THE NEW TESTAMENT

The New Testament presents us with a social pathology that threatens every institution, in particular every religious institution. The conflict of Jesus with the religious institution of his day brings to light more than the personal sins and faults of a few officials; what is revealed is a behaviour of the religious institution, that remains a perpetual temptation to every social organization.

It is recognized quite generally today that the New Testament accounts of the scribes, the pharisees, and the temple priests are not intended as accurate historical descriptions of what these men and their parties were like. We have sufficient information about the various groups and movements in first-century Judaism to realize that the New Testament account does not present a faithful picture of what the men of the Synagogue were like. The evangelists selected their material and proposed it in a manner consonant with the purpose of their books, namely the proclamation of the Good News. Their aim was, in various ways and from different viewpoints, to announce Jesus Christ as the redeemer of mankind, promised in Israel, in whose teaching, life, death, and resurrection God had made himself known as the salvation of men. The details of the gospel accounts all serve this principal intention.

The concern of the evangelists was not history in the modern sense. Even in their representations of Christ's adversaries, their primary concern was not the faithful reproduction of what actually happened but, rather, the revelation, through the things that happened, of what divine redemption means. The struggle of Jesus with the religious institutions of his day has, therefore, a wider meaning for the understanding of the Gospel. Christ's death makes known the power of evil in human life, even though it reveals this in the triumph of God over the enemies of life.

We contend, therefore, that the institution's opposition to Jesus, as recorded in the New Testament, has a message for the Church. We realize that the biblical account reflects, at least in part, the conflicts of the first-century apostolic Church and the religious authorities of the Synagogue. When Jesus argues with his opponents, we also hear the Christian Church arguing with the representatives of the Synagogue. The harshness of some New Testament passages against the people of Jerusalem and their leaders, who are—in the Fourth Gospel—simply called "the Jews," reflects the bitterness which the Church felt against the Synagogue at a later time.

But beyond the conflict between Church and Synagogue, the struggle of Jesus with the institution of his day reveals to us the condition of the Gospel in the world and the blindness which threatens the Christian Church—and every institution. In other words, the struggle of Christ with the religious institution to which he belonged has ecclesiological significance. The struggle reported in the New Testament is part of the divine message that illumines man's present existence. Strangely enough, few theologians have focused their attention on the passage from old to new covenant, and the transition from Synagogue to Church, as an element in the understanding of redemption. It seems to me that in this transition, as presented in the New Testament, we have a revealed basis for a theology of social change. There we learn what is operative in the reform of institutional life and what are the forces that oppose it.

For the first time, as far as I know, this subject has been treated thematically in Yves Congar's important book *Vraie et Fausse Réforme dans L'Eglise*.[13] Here Congar creates a typology of "pharisaism" and "synagogue"—by depicting not what they were like in history but what they stood for in the evangelists' account—which he uses for the understanding of sin in the Church and the resistance of the ecclesiastical government to reform and renewal. The following remarks are largely inspired by Congar's typological thinking.

The reaction of the religious institution to the preaching of Christ contains a divine message for the Church. This, obviously, is not the whole of the divine message, for the Good News for the Church is that Christ, in the power of his Spirit, will always be with her as saviour and mediator to the Father. But Gospel is judgment as well as forgiveness and new life. In Christ's struggle with the religious authorities, as related in the Scriptures, the Church is summoned to self-knowledge.

I must mention in this connection that precisely because the message revealed in the struggle of Jesus with the religious institution was embarrassing to Christians and uncomfortable to the ecclesiastical institution, the Christian Church attempted to ignore it. We did not hear God's Word speaking to us in Christ's conflict with Jewish officialdom. This is the deep reason, it seems to me, why, almost from the beginning, Christians have regarded this conflict as a judgment on the Jews, on the Synagogue, or even the entire Jewish people. Because the Christian Church refused to accept this message and come to self-knowledge, the New Testament was exploited in an anti-Jewish way and became an instrument for the spreading of contempt and moral indignation against the Jewish people. We read the harsh words of Christ addressed to the powerful clique of Jerusalem as a verdict on the Synagogue rather than as the divine disclosure of the temptations that threaten all religious institutions and the dimensions of unbelief among Christians. The anti-Jewishness of the Church's traditional proclamation of the Gospel fulfills, therefore, the classical definition of paranoia: the projection on others of disturbing elements which we do not wish to acknowledge in ourselves. The anti-Semitism of past Christian preaching was an expression of social pathology.

The reasons why the religious institution opposed the preaching of Jesus were complex. Every book of the New Testament sees the problem in a different light. The synoptic gospels distinguish between various parties in Jerusalem, the scribes and pharisees, the sadducees, the temple priests, and attribute different reasons for opposing Christ to each group. The Fourth Gospel no longer distinguishes between these various groups: the opponents of Jesus are grouped together as the powerful clique of Jerusalem and often simply referred to as "the Jews"— a terminology that has had terrible consequences in the centuries that followed. The other writings of the New Testament also present, variously and from differing viewpoints, reasons why the synagogues refused to acknowledge the Gospel of Christ. It is not my intention to analyze this complex picture here. I have done so elsewhere.[14] I simply wish to list some of the reasons why the contemporaries of Jesus rejected his message. These reasons recur as themes in the New Testament and echo the themes found in the prophets of the Old Testament; they explain the people's resistance to God's call.

Here is one reason, then, given in the New Testament, why some people do not believe Christ's message: they do not listen to him. They think they already know the truth. They no longer regard themselves as learners. They insist that God spoke to them in the past. Since truth has been guaranteed to them in their institution, they refuse to listen to Christ's message. The preaching of Christ is unsettling. It threatens the system. To retain a good conscience, many people refuse to listen to him.

When men do not want to listen they always hear what is not being said. They tend to put what is being said to them into their own categories. They reduce the new that is being said to terms which they can handle and which do not threaten the superiority of their own truth. If men are the appointed guardians of truth, they are tempted to hear what has not been said. They interpret a new message in a way not intended by its author. They give a meaning to his gestures which is not there. We read that Jesus was often falsely accused of having taught this or of having done that. Men who regard themselves as knowers and no longer as learners are repeatedly misrepresenting the ideas of others. They are thus justified, in their own eyes, in rejecting them. Men who refuse to listen eventually regard themselves as infallible oracles. Because they say "We see", they reject the truth.[15]

Jesus does not engage in many logical arguments with his opponents. He seems to think that the way in which a message is understood depends largely on the manner of listening to it. Jesus prefers to speak in parables and other literary figures. This manner of communicating brings out more clearly that the true meaning of what is said is lost to the person who is not a listener. As guardians of truth, the men of the institution are tempted to resist the words of Christ.

Here is a second reason for the reaction of the institution to the preaching of Christ. Some people do not listen to the message because they regard themselves as virtuous. They tend to look upon virtue in terms of observance and obedience to rules. Because they follow all that is laid down in law, they think of themselves as just and pleasing to God. This tendency, found in the whole of the human family, is usually called "pharisaism" in Christian literature. The name is unfortunate: it suggests that this was the way in which all pharisees regarded themselves. There is no historical basis for such a judgment. The pharisees had a profound understanding of what holiness is, but they were tempted as are all people, especially religious people, to substitute outer observance for inner devotion.

Because the observance of laws can be achieved by will power, people who fall into "pharisaism" are able to attribute their virtue to themselves. Since will power is the source of this virtue, these men tend to look down on people who do not live up to the norm of morality that is generally accepted. The person who has fallen into the "pharisaic" trap becomes righteous, proud, and judgmental.

Goodness, however, cannot be equated with observance. What counts, ultimately, is the inner disposition of the heart. This is the message of the Old and New Testaments, and this is the conviction of people who are sensitive to the human reality everywhere. The man who regards himself as just and superior to others will have little desire to discover what his heart is really like. If he wants to be comfortable with the image he has made for himself, he will shy away from self-knowledge.

Many contemporaries of Jesus reject his message because they regard themselves as virtuous and refuse to come to deeper self-knowledge. Christ's preaching reveals men to themselves. In his message men discovered that they are sinners and in need of redemption. The encounter with Christ discloses to men not only who he is, but also who they are. Meeting Christ, the man of faith, hope, and love makes other men aware of how different they are from him. Christ makes men face the areas in their lives which are as yet unredeemed. His preaching destroys the self-image of the self-righteous.

When the authorities of Jerusalem meet Jesus, more is involved than their private lives. They represent a class, they stand for an institution, they defend a cause. Their self-image as righteous men is public property. Since their authority among the people depends on this, they promote their own self-image. When they meet Jesus, much is therefore at stake. How can they expose themselves to Christ's preaching and endanger the image of men in authority? The way they interpret their responsibility to the people prevents them from listening to the message and from discovering who they are.

The New Testament describes how Christ's preaching as it comes close to his adversaries, strengthens their defenses: their ears turn deaf and their eyes blind. Truth is threatening to people who do not want to come to self-knowledge. It makes them defensive. It robs them of the power of hearing. For such men it is correct to say that truth closes their ears. This phenomenon is described in the gospels by citing a most revealing passage from the book of Isaiah: "Make the mind of this people gross, dull their ears and besmear their eyes; lest they see with their eyes, and hear with their ears, and have a mind to understand, and turn, and be healed".[16] The truth of God makes deaf men who cling to a self-image that hides who they really are and which is politically useful.

We now come to a third consideration. Many people did not accept the message of Christ because they clung to their position of privilege. The high priests were men of authority in Israel. Since the Romans were the political masters in the land, the power of the high priests had decreased. It was, in fact, rather limited. But as their power became questioned, they became more attached to it and more ready to defend it. This is not unique in the history of institutions. The scribes and pharisees also held positions of honour among the people. They had influence. They were teachers in Israel and as such wore special forms of dress, carried distinctive titles, and enjoyed various social privileges in the community. Jesus described the special place of these men: "They make their stoles broad and the fringes long, they love the place of honour at feasts, the best seats in the houses of worship, and salutations in the market places, and being called 'doctor' by men". Jesus tells his own followers, "You are not to be called 'doctor' for you have one teacher and you are all brethren. Call no one on earth 'father' for you have one Father who is in heaven".[17]

The message of Christ threatens men who cling to their privileges and have special status in the community. What Christ offers a man is to be a brother among brothers. This radical position is at the heart of the Christian Gospel. The great gift that God offers to man in Jesus Christ is to become a man among men, a brother among brothers. The men of the institution who rejected the message thought they had good reasons for clinging to their status. Their privileges were the guarantee of law and order in the community. The special place they held and the honors they received had an important significance for the people. It promoted the common good. These men closed their ears to the message with a peaceful conscience: the institution demanded the defense of their privileges.

The message of Christ threatened a position of privilege on another, more profound level. While the universality of God's love had been made known to the people of the old covenant, it was only in Christ that God revealed the full extent of his mercy in a new and universal covenant. This message could be interpreted as if it meant the loss to Israel of its special position. The early Christians believed that Israel had been elected to be an instrument of salvation for others and hence they did not regard the coming of the new order as a loss to Israel. Israel remained, even in this order, a special instrument of divine salvation. It was the matrix in which the Church took its rise, the ground on which it was founded, and the continuing source of its nourishment.

At the same time, to many people in Israel the message of Christ seemed to destroy their position of divine privilege. These men resented the mercy of God shown to others. This theme is sounded in the synoptic gospels. Jesus deals with it in some of his parables: the peculiar kind of jealousy provoked by unmerited favour shown to others is portrayed in the anger displayed by the elder brother of the prodigal son and the labourers in the vineyard who see the same wages given to those who started work late in the day. Jesus dealt with the same problem from another angle: he asked people who their brother is. The parable of the Good Samaritan makes uncomfortable men who restrict divine brotherhood to their own people.

The same jealousy and attachment to privilege are found in some of the congregations to whom the apostles preached the Good News. This, at least, was the reaction of some Jewish audiences to Paul's preaching as described in the Acts of the Apostles.[18] The Christian message, we are told, made them jealous of the nations of the world to whom the blessings of the covenant were promised without the observance of the Mosaic law. According to the report of the Acts, the local synagogues closed themselves to the Gospel because of their attachment to the privileges of their nation.

We are justified, therefore, in including among the reasons why people opposed the message of Christ, the kind of exaggerated and exclusivist attachment to one's own nation which we call "nationalism" today. This sort of nationalistic feeling, however religious and restrained it may have been at the beginning, existed in the century of Christ. It is clearly revealed in the social hostility between Jews and Samaritans. The book of Acts shows that the distance between Jews and Gentiles was not simply religious but cultural. So great was this cultural difference even in the Church that the tension between Judaeo-Christians and Gentile Christians threatened to undo the unity

THE CREDIBILITY OF THE CHURCH TODAY

of faith and practice and led to the first great crisis in the apostolic community.[19]

Among the reasons why the religious institution resisted the preaching of Christ, we must note another factor. This has to do with the institution's resistance to change. The men of the organization were unwilling to listen to the message of Christ because he announced that in his day God made new and previously unheard-of demands on his own people. The temple clergy and the people who followed them could rightly insist that theirs was a worship divinely appointed, that their ancestors had worshipped God in this manner, and that a respect for their fathers forbade them to change their ways. It was respect and love of the past, of the divinely guided past, that made the hierarchy of Jerusalem unwilling to listen to the message that a new stage in the history of salvation had come and that God revealed himself in a new way, in which he had not spoken to previous generations.

In the name of tradition the institution opposed change. The men in charge were deeply attached to the past. They treasured the gifts of God to his people. Would not a change, possibly a radical change, be a kind of betrayal of their fathers? Should they not serve God in the manner in which they had always done it? Had not previous generations been pleasing to God by following the traditional religion? Their love of tradition was so great that they found it impossible to envisage the possibility that God could be the author of change and initiate people into a new way of serving him.

Some changes in the life of a people are destructive: these changes must be resisted. For this reason, the evangelists used many arguments to show that the changes into which the message of Christ sought to initiate the people were in harmony with what was precious in their past. The transformation announced by Christ did not intend to make the people into another nation. It was intended to lead them to their own proper destiny. In the synoptics Jesus makes a clear distinction between the traditions of men and the Word of God.[20] The Word of God called the people in the desert and united himself to them in a covenant of mercy as the abiding, ever-dynamic reality which was the basis of their peoplehood. This Word must be distinguished from the traditions in which men have interpreted this Word and applied it in various ways to their social existence. Sometimes the traditions of men were so far removed from the Word of God they intended to express, that they were, in fact, at variance with it. It was for the sake of God's Word, then, that the people were asked to separate themselves from the human traditions in their religious and national life. Guarantee of continuity throughout the changes was the ever-dynamic, ever self-identical Word of God. All the evangelists insist that the newness brought by Christ was in harmony with the promises made to Israel in the past. There was no reason, then, to be afraid of change. The change to which Christ summoned his people was not their undoing; it was not accompanied by a loss of identity. On the contrary, the newness of the Gospel initiated people into a change that would be in keeping with their destiny and hence make them more truly what they were meant to be.

Nonetheless, the prospect of change was too frightening for the hierarchy. In the name of tradition the religious institution refused to open itself to the divine message. Instead of heeding the summons to new life in faith it chose to cling to the past, to give new emphasis to its traditions and withdrew from the historical development which promised to take them to their divine destiny.

This brief analysis of why the religious institution in Israel closed itself to the divine message makes it apparent that what happened at the time of Jesus reveals conflicts that occur in other societies, especially religious societies. Resistance to truth, to growth, to newness, to greater recognition of the person and the acknowledgement of fellowship is not proper to the people of first-century Jerusalem. It is not a Jewish issue. It is universal; it happens everywhere; it remains an historical possibility for every society, especially for every religious society.

The analysis we have given also suggests that the forces operative in Jerusalem, producing the resistance to truth, were not simply the personal sins of the leaders but a spontaneous behaviour conditioned by their class and position in society. The New Testament presents us with a description of social pathology. A dynamics at work among those in authority, be they persons or classes, tended to condition men to act in ways in which they would not have acted had their concern been simply private. As men in authority they spontaneously protected their public image. When the powerful groups in Jerusalem refused to be listeners, resisted self-knowledge, and clung to their positions of privilege, preferring the past to the future, they were not making private choices in the freedom of their own hearts; they were men subject to social pressures which they themselves did not understand. According to the biblical account, the authorities who opposed the preaching of Jesus had fallen into the trap that threatens every institution in the world.

THE CATHOLIC CHURCH AND SOCIAL PATHOLOGY

Today we are no longer in need of a long theological justification for applying the conflict of Christ with the religious institution of his day to the life of the Christian Church. While there is a sense in which the Church is indefectibly holy—Christ has identified himself with her—we acknowledge the pilgrim situation of the Church and her vulnerability to failings. Catholics believe that the sacramental liturgy—and this includes the celebration of the Word and the ordination of ministers—is a pledge of Christ's presence and the Spirit's dynamic work in the Church. At the same time we acknowledge the need for perpetual renewal, personal and corporate. One of the achievements of Vatican II—in the face of considerable opposition—was the clear affirmation of the Church as *semper reformanda*. In the *Decree on Ecumenism* we read, "The Church, inasmuch as she is an institution made up of men, is in perpetual need of reformation".[21]

This need for perpetual renewal, we note, is not simply due to the fact that men are sinners. It is not simply the pride and selfishness of people that demand the repeated conversions of the Church. Personal sin is a factor in the Church which demands vigilance, repentance, and the willingness to walk new ways. But the principal reason why the Church is in need of reformation is her existence in history. As she enters into a new historical environment she must adapt herself to the new situation, proclaim the Gospel in a new language and serve the needs of the people in the new age. The same Word of God summons the Church in every age, but in every age this Word makes new demands on her. Listening to God speaking to her in history, the Church must be willing to leave the past behind and enter with Christ into a new future. Even though firmly established in the new covenant, the Church is still in transition, living out the mystery of Christ's presence in the ever-changing ages of history. She must be ready to detach herself from her ties to yesterday's cultures, from the position of privilege she may have enjoyed, from the forms of social organization characteristic of the past, from philosophical traditions that belong to an age gone by, from a style of life that makes her a stranger to the present. Since the Word of God summons the Church to ever-new ways of being faithful to her destiny, the struggle of Jesus with the religious institution of his day is a key for the understanding of the Church's present life.

The New Testament reveals to us the temptations that threaten the institutional Church. This temptation is to resist the living Word of God. As guardians of truth the men of the institution are tempted not to regard themselves as learners. They are tempted to be afraid of the truth and to close themselves to new insights. They are tempted to misunderstand what other people say to them and to attribute to those who disagree with them positions or motives they do not have. The ecclesiastical government is tempted to be deaf to the divine meaning of history and insensitive to the message contained in the experience of the Christian community. In the name of tradition and the divine order of society the hierarchical ministry is tempted to defend its power and privileges, to protect the status quo in the Church, and to advocate conformity and obedience as the great virtues of the Christian people. These remarks do not suggest that the hierarchy necessarily falls into these temptations. The Spirit of God, present in the Church and her government, makes the hierarchical ministry capable of responding to God's Word and —as we shall see—provides dynamic social forces that open the Church to the Spirit and move her with Christ into the future.

It is my thesis that what Charles Davis describes as the ills of the institutional Church is an outline of the social pathology that threatens the Church and every institution in the world. Charles

Davis analyzes the institutional behaviour of the Church in terms of a threefold lack in faith, hope, and love, and maintains that here the Church gives witness against herself. Alas, this social pathology is always present in the Church, as present—we would like to add—as the never-ending manifestations of faith, hope, and love. There is always a kind of ecclesiastical behaviour in the Church that contradicts the Church's Spirit-created being. Despite the institutional gifts of Christ to his people and their protection by his Holy Spirit, the institutional behaviour of the Church remains threatened along the lines made known to us in the New Testament. It is only through the ever-new speaking of God's Word and the ever-new action of the Spirit in the community bringing to life the gifts of Christ made at the beginning, that the Church is perpetually redeemed into being Church. This was true even in the apostolic age. There is always some counter-church in the Church.

Hans Küng expresses this reality in his great ecclesiological studies, in a terminology that is difficult to render into English. As the Germans speak of *Wesen* as the being of a thing and *Unwesen* as the destructive power proper to this being and yet in contradiction to it, so Küng speaks of *Kirche* (Church) and *Unkirche* (possibly rendered by non-church or counter-church) and asserts that *Kirche* is never totally without *Unkirche*.[22] The Church, according to Hans Küng, is always engendered by the Spirit in a situation of *Unkirche*. This means, in our own terminology, that the Church is always created by the Spirit, through institutional gifts or free charisms, in a social situation that is marked by some pathological deformations and, to that extent, testifies against the Church.

These remarks are not meant to reconcile the Christian with the evil in the Church. They are not offered as an excuse for the

Church. They do not intend to cover the suffering and misery which the presence of this social pathology in the Catholic Church produces among people. My point is simply that the counter-witness in the Church is not an argument against her divine mission.

It is my opinion that the Catholic Church has enjoyed few periods in history in which she has been as healthy as today. It has hardly ever been as good in the Church as it is today. We have abandoned most of our political ties. We are detaching ourselves from past cultures. We have entered into a theological and religious pluralism in the Church. There has hardly ever been a time when the Catholic Church has been as willing to come to self-knowledge, to repent of the past and to compare her present life with the possibilities to which Christ in the Spirit is calling her at this time. The courage of the Catholic Church in engaging in self-criticism is a sign of her well-being. It may be that many Catholics today are more aware of the shortcomings of the Church and suffer more from the deformations of her institutional life. But this is not a proof that things are worse today. On the contrary, this is a sign that we realize more intensely what are the real possibilities of the contemporary Church. Stirred up by the renewal in the Church we realize what the Church could be like, we see marvellous manifestations of Christian life within our reach, we feel that the *élan* of renewal could transform the institutional Church into a less imperial and more ministerial body of men. As we compare our realistic hopes with the reluctance to move and the resistance to change on the part of the hierarchy, we feel intense pain, disappointment, anger. The closer men come to freedom, the more they suffer from the remnants of their slavery; the closer men come to self-possession, the more impatient they are with their

80

own failures. The closer men come to the realization of their ideas, the more impatient they become. The present mood of critique and disappointment is, to my mind, a sign that the ecclesiastical renewal has touched the entire life of the Church.

The social pathology in the Church is a universal phenomenon. Every institution is tempted to regard itself as its own end and forget the purpose for the sake of which it exists. This temptation is ever-present. Thanks to the Spirit present to human life there are also other forces at work in institutions, summoning them to health and giving them power of resistance. But whether we look at governments, universities, large companies, agencies of various kinds, we recognize—while appreciating the good and necessary services rendered by them—the possibility and, occasionally, the concrete symptoms of institutional life turning in on itself. The service for the sake of which the institution exists becomes secondary; primary importance is given to promoting its own survival, its own interests, its own power. By a curious inversion of the real situation the institution then comes to look upon the people it is meant to serve, as being there for its own sake. The institution may thus acquire excessive importance in its own eyes, and soon its own authority and influence becomes the criteria by which it judges the life of the entire community. Whatever threatens the superior position of the institution is then regarded as being untrue. The institution may even be tempted to use power against opinions that endanger its superior position. Then the institution will become suspicious of everything new: the new could be a threat. It begins to suspect people with ideas. Every affirmation of life which is not strictly conformist in character is then regarded as subversive. The narcissism into which an institution can fall will eventually lead it to paranoia. It will regard itself as superior to others and suspect the world of plotting against it.

I wish to mention one particular process of social pathology—namely the creation of ideology. According to many contemporary historians every institution creates for itself an ethos, or a teaching on life that is meant to protect the community against others and thus makes it easier for the governing class to assert its power. We may not accept this principle in the strict sense of the Marxist historians. It would be wrong to reduce the ideals, the values, the deep convictions and the faith of a people to an expression of self-interest on the part of society or the governing class. There is no evidence for such a claim. But there is evidence for the more modest claim that the self-interest of society influences the values and ideas which it promotes. Every institution is tempted to create an ideology.

In our day we have become very conscious of the ideologies produced by institutions. We realize that governments are interested in promoting a certain understanding of what it means to belong to the nation, a certain view of loyalty, a certain concept of what other nations are like, and an ethos that makes a radical critique of government policies impossible. We notice such ideologies in universities, in large companies, in medical associations. No institution can totally escape the tendency to present its values and ideals with ideological overtones. The Christian Church is here no exception.

There is good evidence for affirming that the Catholic Church, while gifted with the Spirit and hence faithful bearer of the Good News, is tempted to present its teaching with overtones and emphases that protect the Church from outside influences and make it easier for the ecclesiastical government to rule. The exclusivist understanding of Church, which we held for so long, was strongly influenced by the ideological trend in official teaching. If salvation belongs exclusively to the Church and if the friendship created by the Spirit exists only among members of the Church, then the Church is surrounded by a strong wall, an ideological wall, protecting the people against outside influences. The great stress upon the authority of the hierarchy and the role of obedience in Christian life, and the emphatic proclamation of the infallibility of the magisterium, reflect ideological trends. While Catholics believe that the authority of the ministry and its teaching has its foundation in divine revelation, the emphasis these doctrines were given in the life of the Church were often ideological. They made it easier for the government to rule. We repeat that this is no reflection on the personal holiness of popes and bishops; ideology is a largely unconscious process. Since, in the Catholic Church, government and magisterium are embodied in the same group of men the ideological temptation was, perhaps, greater than in other institutions. In our day Catholics have become sensitive to this. As they listen to the teaching of the hierarchy they ask themselves to what extent is this teaching the proclamation and explanation of the Catholic creed and to what extent is its manner of presentation designed to defend the power of the authorities and protect the present institutional apparatus. The reluctance of the official Church to change its position on birth control is an ideological reaction. If the official position on birth control were changed, it would become more difficult for the ecclesiastical authority to affirm itself. Ideology is always the more or less unconscious defense of the status quo. The ecclesiastical magisterium of the past has overreached itself. In our day popes and bishops have to learn to exercise the doctrinal magisterium more modestly and to promote a theological pluralism in the unity of the Catholic faith.

83

I wish to make a slight digression at this point. It seems to me that in our day the Christian Churches are more healthy than many other societies. The Churches are willing to come to self-knowledge; they are repentent; they acknowledge the need of corporate renewal. This spirit is not always found in other contemporary institutions. Are the universities open to self-criticism and structural reform?[23] It seems to me, rather, that at present the universities often manifest forms of behaviour that have been characterized as pathological in the preceding pages. University authorities sometimes think that the students are there for their benefit. In reality universities are institutions created to serve students and through them the entire community, but through the generation of a certain ethos the university often tends to regard itself as superior to society, initiated into the truth, judging what is highest in life, and hence is too easily inclined to separate itself from the community it is meant to serve. Traditional university boards often look upon students as obedient subjects: until very recently they have shown little inclination to let them participate in policy-making. The same boards find it difficult to let the university cooperate with other social institutions, even other universities, in projects that serve the wider community.

To promote their cause, the universities have created a special ideology. Consciously or unconsciously the universities have devised an image of man that serves as an inspiration for their institution. Man is a purely rational being. Man is a learner of truth. The university in its various departments holds this truth, and as the students faithfully attend the lectures, the appointed professors administer the truth to them. This image of man protects the university and its power. An understanding of man which suggests that the way to truth is different, is often regarded as a threat to the official ideology. The idea that the way to truth involves the whole of man and hence demands participation, growth, and the experience of values, is rejected as unorthodox by many universities. It is accused of not being sufficiently academic, or of offending the objectivity of knowledge, or of being based on positions that are scientifically unverifiable. If professors entertain such critical ideas they may find themselves pushed to the margin of their departments. There are university faculties where the hiring of new teaching staff is dependent on the conformity to an official ideology, avowed or unavowed.

The university is not as unified as it appears. A social dynamics that is not always easy to analyze separates the various departments of the university, even when the subject matter which they study is closely related. Each department develops its own viewpoint, its own language, its own interests. Dialogue across the departmental boundaries is not always easy. It may happen that professors do not understand one another any more. A department of psychiatry in a medical school may have next to no contact with a department of psychology in the faculty of science. More generally the various departments training the helping professions—doctors, nurses, social workers, psychologists, sociologists, possibly even ministers of religion—often have no official conversations, no exchange of views, no pooling of experiences, no ways of learning from one another. While these departments serve man and his well-being in some way, they have often moved so far apart from one another that dialogue and intercommunion become almost impossible.

Shall we take a look at the professors—the ordained ministers —in the life of the university? Who will deny that a social dynamics is at work among them that produces irrational conflicts, power plays, competitions and jealousies that reach deeply into the way men teach and write in their own fields?

Fortunately there are also other social forces at work in the universities that contribute to their well-being. There is a growing concern, at some universities at least, for participation of students, for greater involvement in the life of the community, and for wider inter-departmental conversation and cooperation.

Social pathology, then, threatens all institutions. At the same time, as has been repeatedly suggested, there are also forces at work in society that seek to perfect it, render it more human, and make it a more suitable instrument for promoting the common good and the growth of its members. While there is good reason to be unhappy about the social ills present in all societies, there is also good reason to marvel at the good sense found in societies, at the sanity and peace they express, at the balance and equity they strive for, at the cooperation and understanding they produce. In our first chapter we showed that there is a mystery of reconciliation at work among people. Wherever people are, wherever people live in community and seek to solve their common problems, they are not simply left to their own divisive tendencies: an ecclesial mystery is at work among them enabling them to enter into friendship and common action. Thanks to the presence of God in human life, people are able to grow together in community, serve one another, and foster the well-being of the whole society. Human institutions, therefore, are never totally left to the pathological tendencies present in them; other forces are at work in them, forces due to God's presence to men which draw men into conversation and provide them with new ideas— enabling them to adapt the institutional structure to the needs of human life.

This mystery of new life is present in the ecclesiastical society in a special way. The ecclesial mystery, we believe, will never be overcome in the Church.

What are some of the social processes that bring health to societies? Since the ecumenical movement has been a source of corporate renewal for the Christian Churches, it may be useful to glance at the social dynamics of this movement.

THE ECUMENICAL MOVEMENT

The ecumenical movement has brought the Churches together in conversation and in common projects of social service and missionary witness. It has sought to increase the common ground between the Churches. Dialogue has freed the men involved from inherited prejudices. Making use of common scholarship, Christians found that the doctrinal differences between the Churches are less significant than they had anticipated. Since each Church is willing to seek renewal from the Scriptures, a process has taken place in all the Churches which enables Christians to speak about the Gospel in similar terms, to see the important problems of life in the same way, and to look for solutions in the same direction.

The Christians involved in the ecumenical movement have become advocates of renewal in their own Churches. They began to see traditional positions in a new light. This inevitably provoked a reaction among the more conservative members. The ecumenical movement has caused conversation and even conflict in all the Churches. Men in favour of renewal found themselves opposed by more conservative men deeply attached to the institutional forms of the past. This conversation within each Church, accompanied as it was by some conflict, has made vast numbers of Christians reflect on the meaning of the Gospel and discover for themselves the content of their own Christian convictions. Conflict has been a force of social transformation.

Without attempting to present a complete institutional analysis of the ecumenical movement I wish to mention a few principles of social dynamics that, in my understanding, have had a reforming effect on the Churches and opened them to the guidance of the Spirit. These principles are well known. They belong to the precious experience of many societies today.

The first principle is dialogue with outsiders. A society that engages in dialogue with other societies opens itself to newness and change. Through dialogue we become learners. We get used to listening. We come to realize that we do not know the whole truth. Through conversation with others we not only come to know who they are, we also achieve greater self-knowledge. Dialogue enables us to escape from the self-image which we have created for ourselves and to which we often cling compulsively. Listening to others, facing the reaction which their words have on us, attempting to express to others what is important for us and thus to be known for who we really are—these are ways in which we come to a new self-understanding.

Dialogue with others reveals to us also our misconceptions about them. We are able to discover that many of our prejudices about others are projections of the faults and tendencies which exist in our own group and which we are unwilling to face. Through dialogue we learn to love others. We begin to take seriously their problems and their aspirations. If we discover in dialogue that we have a common purpose and common convictions about what is precious in life, our society will begin to look beyond itself and be concerned with what happens among others.

Dialogue is a remedy for the social narcissism that threatens all institutions.

A second principle of social dynamics, related to the first, is dialogue within the institution. We have mentioned that the experience of the ecumenical movement has shown that dialogue with outsiders inevitably leads to conversation and sometimes to conflict, within the institution. Dialogue has a healing effect on the institution. It brings sections of society into conversation which were isolated from each other. It removes the isolation of the government. It leads to a new openness to truth and eventually enables the entire community to participate in the public decisions that affect their lives.

Participation in policy-making is today regarded as an essential element of healthy social life. There are many forms which this participation can take. Even the Catholic Church, deeply attached to monarchical and authoritarian forms of ecclesiastical government, has modified its position at Vatican II and proposes a collegial ideal of government which, while still retaining certain monarchical principles endorses team-responsibility and the participation of all the members in the making of public policy.

Through the participation of the people, the authorities are protected from forgetting the end for which the institution exists. They are saved from making the institution its own end. Thanks to dialogue and participation the men in authority are subject to criticism, their ideas and programmes are scrutinized, and they have access to the reactions of the people whom they are meant to serve. We have here a social process that is the remedy against the ideological taint that colors the values and the ideas proposed by the authorities. Dialogue is, therefore, necessary even for the utterance of truth.

A third principle of social dynamism, related to the first two, is the cooperation of several societies in a common project. Co-operation goes beyond dialogue. Here institutions engage themselves to strive for the same aim, to plan and work together and even to acknowledge the decisions of other groups in their own policy-making. Cooperation between societies has far reaching effects. It sets up a social dynamics that influences the behaviour and the convictions of the people participating in it. If it is well-conceived it will have the benefits of dialogue. Added to this is the involvement in the concrete order of life. The institutions engaged in common action will begin to experience themselves in a new way. They will understand their own role differently and regard their specific task in a different light. Through cooperation with others, institutions gain a new self-understanding: they grow, they move, they change.

The cooperation of societies in the same project generates social forces that remedy some of the pathological deformations we have described on a previous page. Through cooperative efforts the institutions involved are saved from some of their self-centredness, they are freed from the attachment to their privileges, and they are made sensitive to the needs of the present.

I hasten to add that these social processes are not simply "natural", using the word in its scholastic meaning. These processes are not reducible simply to the human resources of the men involved; they manifest the redemptive or ecclesial mystery present in human life. Through these processes the Spirit is at work in institutions, offering them new life, saving them from their pathologies and enabling them to become more truly what they are meant to be: ministries to the community of men.

Taking the ecumenical movement, in its positive phase, as a model, we have tried to describe some of the social forces that transform institutions and give them access to new life. The ecumenical movement has been the great movement of the Spirit in the Christian world of the 20th century. The movement enabled the Churches to come closer together without compromise. By involving the Churches in reform and renewal it expands the common ground between these Churches. While each Church remains faithful to what it regards as its basic understanding of the Gospel and its divinely guided tradition, ecumenical dialogue and cooperation broaden the area of common faith and practice between them. If this movement continues the Churches may reach a point where their differences no longer seem to them significant or essential. Then the moment has come for starting negotiations for union in a single Church.

This process has gone on among the Protestant and Anglican Churches for two generations and has produced remarkable results. It has gone on for a single generation between the Churches of the Reformation and the Catholic Church. Here, too, the results have been startling. Contrary to the expectation of the skeptical in all the Churches, dialogue and cooperation between Catholics and Protestants has had great effects on the teaching and ecclesiastical policy of the Christian Churches. What has happened in the Catholic Church? The Vatican Council dealt with problems urgent at the time of the Reformation and, reversing the orientation of Trent, sought solutions in the direction advocated by the Reformers. Vatican II adopted the vernacular in the liturgy, it permitted eucharistic communion in two kinds, it stressed the community character of the eucharist, it taught God's redemptive presence in his proclaimed Word, it admitted that the magisterium is not above God's Word but serves it, it affirmed the priesthood created by baptism, it rediscovered the theology of the local Church, it promoted decentralization and ecclesiastical pluralism, it rejected the idea that Scripture and tradition are two independent sources of faith, it affirmed the apostolic witness as the supreme norm of the Church's teaching, it acknowledged the Church's need for an on-going reformation, and it defended the singular dignity of a man's religious conscience.

Can we find similar modifications and developments on the Protestant side? Since the Churches of the Reformation are, on the whole, more loosely organized that the Catholic Church, the developments that have taken place may not be as startling in their effects; but they are just as real. Outstanding among these changes is the new concern for catholic unity. The Protestant Churches have come to acknowledge that visible unity is God's gift to his people and that it is the task of the Churches to make this unity manifest. Protestants have revised the onesidedness of their declarations of protest in the 16th century. They have come to a better appreciation of tradition, they have learnt anew the meaning of sacrament: they no longer think that "Scripture alone" expresses their doctrinal position very clearly, neither in regard to knowledge of the faith nor in regard to its celebration in the community.

The ecumenical movement has, in recent years, made an important discovery. At the beginning of the movement, in the first part of the 20th century, theologians distinguished clearly between doctrine and action. There were theologians, mainly associated with Faith and Order, who insisted that the central effort of the movement must be applied to doctrinal issues. Others, mainly associated with Life and Work, believed that since doctrine is always divisive, the main stress of the movement must be put on common action. This sharp distinction between doctrine and action has marked the entire ecumenical movement.

The discovery of the last decade, perhaps mainly since the Vatican Council, is that the common action of Churches is not simply a service to men in the practical order; it also has a profound effect on the doctrinal understanding of the Churches. Dialogue and cooperation of the Churches in common projects have modified the self-understanding of these Churches and certain doctrinal positions, at one time inacceptable to them, have become valid expressions of their faith.

The Christian Churches have come to realize that doctrines are not abstract propositions with an objective existence beyond history. Doctrines are the expression of the self-understanding of the Churches, created by divine revelation. Doctrines put into words how the Church receives the Word of God and how she understands the redemptive action of the Spirit in her people. Church and doctrine are not two separate realities; doctrine is the crystallization of the Church's self-understanding and hence belongs to the basic reality of what the Church is. The meaning of a particular doctrine is, therefore, not grasped as a non-historical statement of truth; it is grasped only in the context of the entire self-understanding of the Church in history. Catholics believe, we may add, that this self-understanding is measured by the apostolic tradition present in the Scriptures and guided by the Holy Spirit, the normative expression of which is, ultimately, the work of the bishops and the pope.

The experience of the ecumenical movement verifies that the Churches entering upon a new self-understanding—through dialogue and cooperation—reinterpret their doctrinal positions in the light of the new understanding of themselves. In other words, common action among Christians is not a purely practical affair; it has, in fact, profound doctrinal consequences.

This re-interpretation of traditional doctrinal positions is best illustrated from the experience of the Catholic Church at Vatican II. Because the ecumenical movement, a wider dialogue with the modern world, and the experience of dialogue and conflict at the Council itself had introduced the Catholic Church into a new understanding of herself, of her role in the world and her relation to other Churches, she was able to reinterpret certain traditional positions in the light of this new self-understanding. The Church radically modified her exclusivist position. At Vatican II Catholic doctrine changed. The Church spelled out in a new way what other people were to her—Christians, Jews, members of other religions and people in general. Doctrinal positions which at a time not so far away had been regarded as irreconcilable with the Catholic faith, were adopted by the Vatican Council as doctrinal expressions of the Church's new self-understanding.

This recent discovery of the ecumenical movement means that there may not be static block of doctrinal positions that will keep the Churches forever apart. The scholarly dialogue that has been carried on for several decades has freed the Churches from prejudice, purified their doctrinal formulations from ideological overtones, and enriched their doctrinal understanding by a return to the Scriptures. While this scholarly dialogue widened the common ground between the Churches, it eventually had to face a solid block of doctrine that stood between the Churches. The recent discovery of the ecumenical movement has brought to light the limitations of this scholarly dialogue. What is more important than this dialogue for a future doctrinal consensus of the Churches is their collaboration, on all levels, in common projects. What counts is the engagement of the Churches in a common mission. This kind of dialogue and cooperation, involving people on all levels of church life, generates a new self-understanding of the Churches and thus enables them, eventually, to re-interpret those doctrinal positions which, at present, separate them. The new discovery of the ecumenical movement makes new demands on the Christian Churches. Common ecclesiastical action, participation in the same mission, cooperation in the same educational institutions, collaboration in the same pastoral projects—these are the manifestations of ecumenism today. In the past, we may have passed these efforts off as being simply "practical", not "theological" enough; today we realize that this common action is an ecclesial action that has profound effects on the doctrinal positions of the Churches. The action of the Church re-situates her in history, and from the new perspective she will formulate the unchanging Gospel by re-interpreting her traditional teaching.

What I have called the new discovery of the ecumenical movement, verified especially at Vatican II, makes the hope for Christian unity more realistic. The life of the Churches may prove that there is no lasting doctrinal block separating them. This new discovery, we note, is not fully appreciated in some traditional ecumenical environments where doctrines are still regarded as true propositions independent of the Church's life, and hence where ecumenical dialogue is understood mainly in intellectual terms. The new discovery is also underestimated by certain avant-garde theologians who regard ecumenism as naïve and unrealistic and who wish to rush into the future without preserving the continuity of the Church through the evolution of her own self-understanding.

We conclude that the ecumenical movement which widens the common ground between the Churches has, through its social processes, such a profound effect on the participating Churches that the doctrinal obstacles to unity, existing between them, could be overcome without compromise and without conversion.

Since this development—if it is to come about—lies in the future, it is impossible at this time to say what the one Church of reconciliation will be like. All we know is that it will be in essential continuity with every Church that joins the reconciliation. The Christian who belongs to this one Church will not regard it as a new Church but as his Church, the Church to which he has always belonged, the Church in continuity with what was most precious in its own past.

After examining the social pathology in the Church, especially in the terms revealed to us in the New Testament, we have studied the ecumenical movement as a model of social processes that transform societies and save them from their sickness. We have chosen the ecumenical movement because it has demonstrated in our own lifetime its power to affect ecclesiastical institutions and its hold on the minds of the Christian people. The ecumenical movement has been a movement of the Spirit in the Churches. That is to say that the social processes which the movement has produced were operative in the Churches themselves. They are examples of the social processes by which the Spirit heals the Churches from their pathological patterns. They illustrate that what is required for the reform of the Churches is not the personal conversion of bishops and popes to greater holiness—this may not have any direct effect on public policy and teaching; what is required, rather, is the introduction of new social processes which open the Church to the Spirit and enable her to give up its pathological attachments to the past.

We must still look more closely at the ecumenical movement. Until now we have dealt only with its positive phase, its power to transform societies. Yet since this movement is a reality in history it is inevitably ambiguous and hence is threatened, in its own way, by what we have referred to as social pathologies. We will have to look at some of the criticism that has been raised against ecumenism by contemporary Christians.

It has been suggested that the ecumenical movement tends to isolate Christians from the rest of the world. Christians coming together in the search for unity have formed a new ideological community that has closed itself off from other people. Having removed the walls from around the Churches, ecumenism has erected them around the Christian community as a whole. What has been the effect of this new isolation?

Instead of helping one another to leave the past behind and step courageously into the future, the ecumenical movement could foster in us our fear of the present and offer us an escape into a happier past. At ecumenical gatherings we studied the past, we used the same historical methods in understanding the past, and hence—in the new mood—we have come to agree on what happened in the past, even in the controversial periods of Church history. Protestants and Catholics find that they can settle certain issues that divided them in the 16th century. Will this help us to return to the undivided Church of the West prior to the Reformation? Catholics and Orthodox, examining the past in an ecumenical spirit, may also find common roots and basic agreement in their ancient history. Will this enable us to return to the undivided Church of the early centuries? I hope not. For what is demanded of the Church—as of any society—is to deal with the present. The ecumenical movement may tempt the Church to look to the past for the solution of present problems. What the ecumenical movement should do and wants to do is to enable the Churches to face the issues of the present in unison so that together, in search of greater fidelity to Christ, they may create their new future.

Another criticism has been raised. The ecumenical movement,

because of its isolation from the world, could multiply the pathological difficulties in the Churches.[24] Since the Christian Churches do not only share a common Gospel but also have a common burden of structural problems, since, in fact, the pathological patterns that have contributed to the original divisions have marked the Churches from their beginning, it is possible that, coming together in the ecumenical movement, they confirm one another in their pathological patterns. The ecumenical movement, some have suggested, in addition to all the good it has done, has also strengthened the Churches in some of those elements that obscure the Gospel in the world. In other words, the ecumenical movement has been accused of re-enforcing the ideological trends of the Christian Churches.

Here is an example. Learned and painstaking dialogue on the ministry, extending over a long period, could have an ambiguous effect on all the Churches. By concentrating on this problem, the existing ministry in each Church becomes a more clearly defined caste, conscious of its own position, with definite privileges, insisting on its separateness, while it should be the effort of all the Churches to deepen the fellowship between Christians, baptised and ordained. While the ecumenical discussion on the ministry may bring to light a wider area of agreement on the subject, the over-all effect of this discussion would be negative if, in fact, it widened the gap between the people and their ministers in the Church. The widening of the gap between the people and the institutions serving them is one of the basic pathological trends threatening all societies. Could it not happen, then, that by dealing with the ministry in a context restricted to the Churches, the ecumenical movement in fact strengthens the ideological trends in each of them?

The Christian critics of the ecumenical movement have sug-

gested that in the quest for unity today dialogue and cooperation must be extended to people and groups beyond the baptismal
covenant. In other words, they advocate that the ecumenical
movement include non-Christians in its conversation and common action. This is often called "secular ecumenism". Secular
ecumenism insists that the ecumenical movement is in need of
correctives and guidance that are supplied by the Spirit through
a widening of perspectives. The presence of other people in
ecumenical conversation and association will prevent Christians
from running away into the past and from choosing problems for
discussion that allow them to escape from reality. Ecumenical
dialogue in which other people and other groups participate will
detach the Christian Churches from their privileges and make
them aware of their own ideological trends. Extending ecumenical conversation to men who do not acknowledge the special
status of the ministry may save the ecclesiastical hierarchy from
seeing things in the perspective of those exercising authority.
Who would not wish to see the first bishop and other princes
of the Church put on a sport shirt, smoke a pipe, and attend discussion groups in the secular world? The advocates of secular
ecumenism do not deny that Christians have to come together
among themselves to deal with the issues of doctrine and church
order. But they insist that the general orientation of the ecumenical movement must be toward dialogue and cooperation
with the world. The presence of other people in ecumenical
conversation makes the Churches deal with problems that are
problems to the whole world and enables them to come to grips
with present reality. This wider dialogue is necessary to deliver
the ecumenical movement from turning in on itself.

Secular ecumenism has a sound doctrinal basis. The Church
needs the world to become Church. Since God addresses men

from within their lives, wherever they may be and offers them new life, the Church who wishes to be obedient to God must listen to his Word in the Scriptures, in her own life, past and present, and in the experience of mankind. Since God has redemptively involved himself in the whole of mankind the Church that wants to be open to this redemptive mystery must be in dialogue with people everywhere. In other words, the Church needs other people, the whole experience of mankind, to find her unity and become more truly herself.

We have seen that Charles Davis' negative evaluation of the Catholic Church has led us to a wider theological consideration of subjects that have often been neglected in Christian thought. The Gospel reveals the ambiguity of human society. Forces destructive of human well-being are operative in it. At the same time, the Gospel reveals that the Spirit is present wherever people are, and that social processes are, therefore, available by which institutions are saved from their pathologies and made into healthier expressions of men's life in community. For centuries theologians have interpreted the Gospel in terms of what happens to the individual: we teach the ambiguity of man, his sinfulness, his need of redemption; we proclaim salvation in terms of conversion, forgivenness of sin, and new life. Grace, in this theological tradition, is understood in terms of personal transformation. But since God is redemptively present to the whole of human history, is it not necessary to understand grace also in terms of social transformation? We have as yet hardly a theology of sin, conversion, and new life which is applicable to societies.

Johannes Metz has given a special name to the tendency of understanding the Gospel in terms of what happens to individuals: he has called this "the privatization of the Gospel".[25] Metz advocates "the de-privatization" of Christian theology. He insists that it must be the effort of theologians today to interpret the meaning of the Gospel, both as judgement and grace, for man's social life in history. Metz calls this "political theology".[26] The Christian regards the Gospel not simply as a key for the understanding of personal life; he must learn to look upon it also as the key for the understanding of social life. Ecclesiology is, therefore, not simply a study dealing with the Christian Church; it is a study dealing with the whole of man's social existence in history. Ecclesiology reveals to us the ambiguity of institutional life as well as the social processes by which the Spirit is present to society. Since this chapter deals with the Gospel as social critique, it is a modest contribution to political theology.

3.

The Apologetics of Yesterday

In this chapter I wish to examine the customary arguments for the credibility of the Catholic Church. This chapter, in other words, deals with apologetics. I have no intention of raising the entire issue of apologetics in this context, even though such a study would be of great importance today. In recent years Catholic theologians have shied away from the subject. The highly rationalistic apologetics created in the 19th century and dominant in our religious manuals right into the present century has become discredited in the intellectual climate created by the contemporary theological renewal. A deeper appreciation of God's Word as power has made the apologetical issue less important. God communicates himself in his Word proclaimed and celebrated in the Church and it is he who, in his Spirit, creates the response of faith in those who listen. This recovery of a theology of revelation has diverted the interests of pastors from apologetics to liturgy and catechetics. God himself, in his Word, provides the foundation of belief. Catholics have become convinced that the revealed faith is handed on and defended, not by perfecting a system of apologetics but by proclaiming the Word in a manner that can be understood by people and by celebrating it in meaningful sacramental worship.

At the same time we cannot avoid the apologetical issue altogether. Even if we believe that God's Word addresses us in power and that God's Spirit creates in us the response of faith, this faith in us is, nonetheless, a human reality. It is a human commitment, and hence is both free and responsible. No insistence on the gratuitous and divine character of this faith dispenses us from looking at it as a human reality, part of a man's rational life, and from inquiring into the human reason for believing. Apologetics, as the study of the human "why" of believing, remains the task of theology.

The apologetics of the 19th century was characterized by the radical distinction between faith and its rational credibility. This distinction was the brilliant attempt, endorsed by the ecclesiastical magisterium, to steer a middle course between two opposing intellectual trends that were regarded as threats to the Catholic Church. On the one hand, a highly rationalistic trend wished to demonstrate the truth of the Christian Gospel and make faith the certain conclusion of a rational argument, and on the other, a so-called fideistic trend denied the rational foundation of belief altogether and simply looked upon the religious experience of men in the encounter with the Scriptures and the life of the Church as the human foundation of the Christian faith. Against theological rationalism, the Catholic Church affirmed the gratuitous character of faith. Faith is a gift. Faith is beyond man. Faith can never be demonstrated. Against fideism—at least, as it was interpreted by the authorities—the Catholic Church defended the rational character of the human commitment which is faith. The surrender to God's Word in faith can be defended as a reasonable choice before the objective bar of reason.

To steer the middle course between these two trends, Catholic theology introduced the radical distinction between faith and its credibility. Faith was the acknowledgement of God's Word in the message. Faith was the acceptance of the message as the divine utterance. The credibility of the message was the rational demonstration, based on historical documents and the miracles recorded in them, proving its divine authorship. The message to be believed was regarded as rationally credible because a reliable historical record affirmed its divine origin, and miracles associated with the message and recorded in the same records demonstrated this divine origin. According to this theory, then, faith and credibility belonged to altogether different cognitive orders. With the help of this distinction, therefore, Catholic theology of the 19th century, largely supported by the First Vatican Council, was able to assert the indemonstrable and totally gratuitous character of faith—against the rationalist—and at the same time defend—against the fideists—the rational foundation of this faith, that is, its credibility as rationally demonstrable. In this way apologetics became the science of the credibility of faith! It attempted to work out arguments and proofs that defended the rational foundation of the Christian faith before the world of unbelievers. Even the arguments for the credibility of the Catholic Church intended to demonstrate to unbelievers the divine authorship of the Church's message about herself. This was done either by providing an historical demonstration that this Church was founded by Jesus Christ, or by proving that some of the characteristics of the Church's life were miraculous and hence pointed to her divine foundation.

The radical distinction between faith and credibility has been abandoned by the vast majority of Catholic theologians today. Ever since Maurice Blondel's famous *Letter on Apologetics* published in 1896, the entire apologetical effort of the 19th century has been severely challenged in the Catholic Church. It is generally recognized today that the credibility of the faith— however understood—is acknowledged by the same *élan* of a man's mind by which he opens himself to God's Word and his saving wisdom. The notion of rational credibility, in the technical sense of the 19th century apologetics, has been largely abandoned. It is a question today whether to preserve the word "credibility" and give it a new meaning in the study of apologetics, or whether to drop the very term and find another word which better expresses the factor of rationality in Christian faith.

Since Charles Davis has raised the question of credibility, at least in part, in the traditional context, we must deal with the traditional arguments which sought to establish the credibility of the Catholic Church. As I have indicated above there are basically two sets of arguments. The first is historical, the *via historica*. The theological authors attempted to show from the Scriptures and the early history of the Church that Jesus Christ founded a visible society, and that this society is none other than the Catholic Church. To do this these authors tried to show, from the historical records, that Jesus chose twelve apostles as the foundation of the Church, that among them he gave a special place of leadership to Peter, that he intended that the power of the apostles to teach and to rule be handed on to their successors the bishops, and among them to the successor of Peter, the pope, as supreme teacher and ruler. This society is the Catholic Church.

A second proof approaches the problem from an examination of the present situation. The Christian finds himself surrounded by many Christian Churches. He wants to find the true one among them. The Catholic apologists tried to show that the true Church, according to the New Testament witness, has certain marks identifying her, namely unity, catholicity, holiness, and apostolicity, and that these marks are found today only in the Catholic Church. The Catholic Church must therefore be the Church of the New Testament. These marks, the apologists tried to show, have a miraculous and hence supra-human character. They indicate even to the unbeliever that the Catholic Church is of divine origin. This argument was called the *via notarum*. We shall examine the *via historica* and the *via notarum* in the light of contemporary Catholic thought.

PROOF FROM HISTORY

In his *A Question of Conscience* Charles Davis rejects the historical argument for the credibility of the Church. He realizes that in doing so he simply follows the biblical and historical scholarship which is accepted by all students of Christian antiquity today. We have come to realize the complexity of the New Testament. We have come to realize the diverse ecclesiastical traditions reflected in the New Testament, the variety of ministries described, and the slow and uneven evolution to which the Bible and the other historical records give witness. Today it is generally admitted that no Christian Church can demonstrate the apostolic origin of its ecclesiastical structure from the pages of the New Testament.

Recent scholarship in the Catholic Church—I wish to refer here especially to the vast historic research of Hans Küng in his most recent study *The Church*—has brought some clarity into the complex issue of the Church's historical origins. There is much evidence that the story of the twelve who transmit their apostolic powers by the laying on of hands or the ordination

of bishops is a symbolic account in which the Church announces
the guidance of the Spirit in the structural evolution that has
taken place over a considerable period of time.[1] The New Testament testifies, for instance, that the apostleship was at first not
limited to the twelve. Paul was an apostle. So was Barnabas.[2] A
doctrinal development, recorded by Luke, made the Church
speak exclusively of the "twelve apostles".[3] It has been shown,
furthermore, that the first meaning of apostolic succession had
reference, not to particular individuals in the Church but to the
entire community of the Church. "Apostolic, i.e. in succession
of the apostles, is the entire Church when she keeps, in all her
members, fidelity to the witness of the apostles as well as the
connection with the ministry of the apostles."[4] This apostolic
ministry in the early Church was manifold. We have, for instance, quite diverse ministries in the Church of Jerusalem and
in the Pauline communities. A slow development, partly recorded in the New Testament itself, led to the threefold ministry
of bishop, presbyter, and deacon that we eventually find in the
universal Church.

Hans Küng, in his study, has tried to trace this development
in the early Church. From the beginning the ministries in the
Church were complex. "God has appointed in the Church first
apostles, second prophets, third teachers, then, workers of miracles,
then healers, helpers, administrators, speakers in various kinds of
tongues."[5] Küng is able to show that the charismatic ministries
of prophet and teacher remained in the early Church for a considerable period of time and that the apostolic structure of the
Church remained flexible and adaptable long after New Testament times. These diverse ministries in the Church were all regarded as apostolic.[6]

The bishops were called the successors of the apostles because they inherited the exclusive charge of the apostolic ministry and thereby embodied the apostolic succession of the entire Church. Küng writes, "The apostolic succession of the entire Church expressed itself more clearly as the apostolic succession of a particular ministry, especially when, at the end of the second century the prophets, and in the third century also the free teachers in the community had largely disappeared and thus also the teaching function was exercised more and more by the bishops and their helpers. In the community of the faithful, born of the collegiality of all believers, of all bearers of charisms and ministries, that is, born of the collegiality of the entire Church as such, emerges more strongly the collegiality of a particular ministerial body within the community: the collegiality of the bishops (*episcopoi-presbyteroi*)."[7] A similar process, which can be traced in part, permits the emergence of the monarchical episcopate out of the collegiality of several bishops (*episcopoi-presbyteroi*) in the congregation.[8]

In the same study Hans Küng shows how these results of modern scholarship have already influenced the composition of the conciliar documents at Vatican II.[9] In particular he compares the canon of the Council of Trent, "Whoever says that in the Catholic Church there is no hierarchy appointed by divine ordination, consisting of bishops, presbyters, and deacons, let him be anathema",[10] with the more careful formulation of the Vatican Council. This formulation refers to the Tridentine canon in a footnote but, in fact, slightly modifies its position. According to Vatican II, "The divinely established ecclesiastical ministry is exercised on different levels by those who, from antiquity, have been called bishops, priests and deacons".[11] We note that while the Tridentine canon seems to apply the divine ordination to the threefold hierarchy, the Vatican text speaks of divine

108

THE APOLOGETICS OF YESTERDAY

institution only in reference to the ecclesiastical ministry in general. We note furthermore that while the Tridentine canon claims that this hierarchy consists of bishops, priests, and deacons, the Vatican text merely says that the ecclesiastical ministry "is exercised" by those who "from antiquity"—that is, not from the beginning—have been "called" bishops, priests, and deacons.

It is impossible to prove the hierarchical system of the Catholic Church from the New Testament. The historian is able to trace a development, recorded in the New Testament, in which different forms of ministry gave way to new forms that would assure the unity of the local congregation and the unity of the universal Church. This development continues in the age after the formation of the New Testament, but it remains in harmony with the biblical meaning and purpose of the ministry. Since the Catholic Church regards herself as the community of the Spirit and hence has a special understanding of her own history or tradition, she is able to affirm that her own ecclesiastical structure, the episcopal college and its head the pope, is the divinely appointed ministry through which Christ is made present in the Church. It is, therefore, not on a critically evaluated historical basis that the Church defends the divine appointment of her ministry; it is, rather, the self-understanding of the Church in faith that enables her to affirm that her ecclesiastical ministry is the gift of Christ through the Spirit. A secular scholar may trace the complex historical development of the ministry through the apostolic age and beyond, but if he does not acknowledge the presence of the Spirit in the Church he will not attach the same value as a Catholic to the consensus of the Church that this development was in keeping with the apostolic witness and the sense of the Scriptures and hence it was, in fact, the work of the Spirit.

We might mention that this development is already outlined

in the New Testament. The pastoral epistles present this evolution at a fairly late stage. Because of this, we may add, the Protestant Churches find it equally impossible to defend their own ministerial structures simply from the historical evidence provided by the New Testament.[12]

The ecclesiastical ministry in the Catholic Church of today is quite different from the ministry in the apostolic Church and even from the ministry in the early Church after the general emergence of the monarchical episcopate. The evolution of the papacy in later centuries—here, too, the growth was tested by the Scriptures and confirmed by consensus—and the understanding of ecclesiastical power in terms of "jurisdiction" has given the Catholic hierarchy the image of "princes of the Church", an image that is confirmed in their titles and ornaments. Few Catholic theologians today will assert, therefore, that the credibility of the Catholic Church can be demonstrated on the basis of purely historical analysis of the Church's origin. The believing Catholic—who has accepted the Church in his Christian faith—will study the history of the beginnings and see in it a development in which the Spirit was involved. It is faith that makes the Catholic acknowledge the growth of the Church as the work of the Spirit. It is faith in Christ's perpetual presence in the community of the faithful that enables the Catholic to look at the complex history of early Christianity and recognize in the development that brought about the ecclesiastical ministry the guidance of Christ's Spirit, in keeping with the written record of the apostolic age. The Catholic Church believes, therefore, that her hierarchical ministry is the legitimate heir and successor of the apostolic ministry—despite the obvious differences between the two and despite the present need of reform—according to an historical development that was tested by the Scriptures and approved, in the Spirit, by the whole community.

At the same time the Catholic Church must continue to test her ministry by the apostolic witness. We can never turn away from the New Testament to some later period. The New Testament is the record of the apostolic preaching and, as such, remains normative for the entire teaching and practise of the Church in later centuries.[13] In her teaching and practise the Church serves the Word of God as present to her in the Scriptures.

What does the Church learn from the Scriptures in regard to her hierarchical ministry? I shall simply mention three points. First, the Scriptures offer us a message of what ministry is. This remains Word of God for us, by which we must always correct ourselves. The Scriptures reveal to us how the ministry in the Church is threatened, how it can be abused, how power can corrupt, how it can divide the Church. Christ tells us that ministry is service. Ministry does not disrupt brotherhood in the Church. Ministry is not a caste in the Church. Ministers do not behave like princes in the Church. Ministry serves the unity, the fellowship, and well-being of the entire body of the faithful. It is by this scriptural message about what ministry is, that the ecclesiastical ministry of any age, including the present, must always test itself. In this sense the New Testament is the norm of all ministry in the Church.

Secondly, the study of the New Testament teaches the Church the extraordinary flexibility of the apostolic ministry. The early Church knew several patterns of ministry. The early Church even acknowledged a role for a ministry that was charismatic and non-official. The form of ministry was adapted to the needs of people and the changing conditions of the culture in which

111

they lived. The highly diversified non-hierarchical ministry in the Pauline Churches was as authentically apostolic as the hierarchical structure of the Church in Jerusalem. Without attempting to return to an earlier period of her history, the Christian Church is always able to move ahead in adapting her ministerial structure to the changing needs of the people and the conditions of present day life. While the Catholic believes that the present hierarchical structure of the Church embodies the divinely appointed ministry, he may also be convinced that the feudal structure of this ministry and the authoritarian ways adopted in the age of monarchy are phases that should be left behind. Some Catholics assert that these phases *must* be left behind if the Church wants to exercise her mission in the present world.[14]

Thirdly, the Catholic Church learns from the New Testament that apart from the officially recognized ministry there may be other ministries, charismatic and out of the ordinary, through which God nourishes his people. In the Church of the first two centuries the official ministry was usually accompanied by other forms of ministries, more free and adaptable and not organizationally dependent on the official ministry. These charismatic ministries were also apostolic.[15] For this reason, the Catholic Church, which believes in the divine appointment of her bishops in apostolic succession and the priests in dependence on them, need not exclude the possibility that there be other ministries, the origin of which is more charismatic and out of the ordinary, which, also, deserve the name of apostolic. In other words, the confrontation with the New Testament enables the Catholic Church, which affirms the unique validity of her own ministerial hierarchy, to open her mind to the possibility that the ministries in the other Christian Churches which, while possibly not in strict historical apostolic succession may deserve, because of their charismatic origin and the present call of God, to be called apostolic. In this important ecumenical problem the New Testament witness offers the Church a flexibility which she has not hitherto realized.

THE PROOF FROM THE FOUR MARKS

The second traditional argument demonstrating the credibility of the Catholic Church deals with the signs by which a person in the present may detect the true Church of Christ in the world, namely with the signs of the Church as one, catholic, holy, and apostolic.

The ancient Church regarded itself as one, catholic, holy, and apostolic. These adjectives proclaimed the work of the Spirit in the Church. It is by faith that the Christian acknowledges—and professes in his creed—that the Holy Spirit is present in the community of the faithful, that he unifies this community in the diversity of its life, that he applies the forgiveness of Christ and makes her holy, and finally that he makes the Church as well as her ministry faithful to the apostolic witness and origin. These Spirit-produced properties of the Church—that is, unity, catholicity, holiness, and apostolicity—were occasionally regarded as visible marks certifying her mission in the world. It was only during the Reformation that the consideration of the four properties mentioned in the creed, was transformed into an apologetical demonstration of the true Church in contrast to the other, the "false" Churches which then surrounded the Catholic Church.[16] The attempt was made to demonstrate the credibility of the Catholic Church by showing that in her we find unity and universality, holiness and apostolic tradition as in no other Church.

113

The Protestants of that period presented their own apologetical proofs. They also taught that there were notes of the true Church which help Christians to detect her among the various ecclesiastical communities. True Church was the congregation where the Word was truly preached and the sacraments rightly administered. The Protestant authors tried to show that this happens only in the Churches of the Reformation. In the Catholic Church, they said, the Word was no longer preached in its purity: doctrines had been added. The sacraments, further, were not celebrated according to the Scriptures: for instance, eucharistic communion was served only in one kind.

Catholic authors had no objections against the marks of the true Church as defined by the Protestants. Since Catholics thought that the Word was purely preached and the sacraments rightly administered in the Catholic Church, they believed that these two signs were present in the Catholic Church and hence that they could hardly serve as distinguishing marks. At the same time the Protestants also acknowledged that the true Church of Christ was one, holy, catholic, and apostolic, and in their conflict with the Spirituals, the so-called radical wing of the Reformation, they insisted that these four properties were present in the Protestant Churches.

In the 19th Century Catholic authors in conflict with the world of unbelievers and rationalists developed a proof for the credibility of the Catholic Church based on the four marks. They tried to show that these four marks are visible signs of miraculous character, present in the Church. In a world where disunity, particularity, sinfulness, and instability dominate human life and threaten every institution, every nation, every religion, the triumph over these destructive forces in the visible unity, universality, holiness, and apostolicity of the Catholic Church is a sign of supra-human dimension. These marks were presented as miraculous signs vouching for the divine origin of the Church and her message. This is the *via notarum* which is found in the manuals of religion right into the 20th century.

This twofold use of the four notes, as visible signs of the true Church contesting the Protestant claims and as miraculous signs of social life challenging the unbeliever, made great demands on the Catholic apologist. It tempted him to present the Church's past history as well as her present reality in the world in an apologetical way. He covered over her shortcomings and depicted in most advantageous fashion the success of the Church as the undivided and universal community, dedicated to holiness and faithful in teaching and ministry to the apostolic witness. The apologist was always under a strain. He was always afraid that a more realistic study of history and a closer look at present ecclesiastical life would destroy the fourfold image he had constructed. Remnants of this approach to church history remained with us until recently.

A considerable change occurred in apologetics through the progress of ecclesiology in the 20th century. The great theologians of our time who dealt with the mystery of the Church regarded the four properties mentioned in the creed, as belonging to the essence of the Church as it is being produced by Christ in the Spirit and acknowledged, in the same Spirit, by the faithful. Contemporary ecclesiology presents the four properties as descriptions of the redemptive communion which, despite the sinfulness of men, the Holy Spirit keeps on producing in the midst of the faithful, through the hierarchical ministry as well as through the faith, hope, and love of all Christians. In this manner a more profound understanding was obtained of what unity means, of what catholicity, holiness, and apostolicity mean, and

115

it became clear in the contemporary theological literature that the four characteristics of the Church were gifts as well as challenges to the Church. Christ, in the Spirit, is at work among Christians: uniting them in a single fellowship of faith, hope, and love (unity), freeing them to become more truly themselves according to their personal talents and their particular culture in the unity of faith (catholicity), forgiving sins and producing new life through the celebration of Word and liturgy (holiness), and preserving the entire Church in the apostolic faith, once for all delivered to the saints, through the work of the Spirit in each member and the special assistance of the hierarchy in historical succession with the apostles (apostolicity). These four marks, then, are God's gifts to the Church. They are present in the Church through God's gift of himself in the Spirit, and they are institutionally rooted—Catholics believe—in the doctrinal, sacramental, and ministerial gifts of Christ to his people.

At the same time these four marks are challenges to the Church. They judge us. They tell us what the Church must always become. They reveal to us how the Spirit is summoning us to conversion. They make known to us what Jesus is doing in our midst, and disclose the measure of our resistance to him. These four marks, therefore, must be understood as gift and as challenge, or, as the Germans say, as "*Gabe*" and "*Aufgabe*", which the faithful acknowledge with joy, with repentance and with hope.

This deeper understanding of the four qualities of the Church made their apologetical use extremely difficult. If they are described as miraculous signs visibly present in the Church, they cease to be the promises of God which challenge the Church, judge the quality of ecclesiastical life, and stir up the entire Christian community to greater fidelity to the Spirit. A presentation of these four qualities as visible marks, moreover, demanded that preference be given to the external aspects of these qualities. Unity was then understood mainly in institutional terms: the Church is one in defined doctrine. Catholicity was then described mainly in geographical terms: the Church is catholic in her extension. Holiness was then defined mainly in liturgical terms: the Church is holy in her sacramental liturgy. Apostolicity was understood mainly in terms of the hierarchy: the Church is apostolic in her bishops in apostolic succession. Modern ecclesiology has brought out the ambiguity of these external manifestations. The theologian may not look at the four properties of the Church by concentrating on their external aspects. His task is, rather, to show that these external manifestations do not necessarily correspond to an inner reality. Institutional unity may cloak the lack of vital communion, it may cover up deep divisions about what is important in the Gospel, it may hide indifferentism and the lack of faith. The geographical universality of the Church may cloak an aggressive spiritual colonialism; it may hide a successful attempt to impose the religious culture of one continent on other peoples. Holiness understood in terms of sacramental life may cloak formalism, legalism, and a multitude of sins. And the historical succession of bishops in an unbroken chain from apostolic times need not recommend the apostolicity of their message nor of their style of leadership. Because the four marks are both gifts and challenges, the Catholic theologian of today will hesitate to use them as visible notes whereby to show that the Catholic Church is the true Church of the Lord. Since we have become conscious of the shortcomings of the Church and realize more than ever the need of repentance and divine forgiveness, contemporary Catholics have little sympathy for the

117

attempt to demonstrate the credibility of their Church by the *via notarum*.

Some apologists have reduced the consideration of the four marks to a single one, namely the Church's apostolicity. These authors have tried to show that the Catholic Church stands in direct and unbroken continuity with the Church of the apostles, especially because of papal primacy. This is the *via primatus*. While admitting the later development of the central position of the bishop of Rome, these authors were able to point to a wide scriptural tradition acknowledging the special position of Peter among the apostles and in the early Church. The form critical approach to the Scriptures strengthens this argument. The references to the Petrine primacy in several gospels and other New Testament writings indicate much more than the memory of the single biblical authors; they reflect, rather, the living conviction of the Churches in which these various parts of the New Testament were composed. There can be no doubt that the passages expressing the prime position of Peter reflect the consciousness of the early community that Peter was given a special role and that this role continued to have meaning in the Church after his disappearance. The structural developments of the papacy that took place later on, in part influenced by the central position of Rome in the ancient world, was tested by the Scriptures and approved by the growing Church to be the fulfillment of the promises which the apostolic Church, in a variety of contexts, remembered in regard to Peter. A good case can be made for regarding the apostolic succession of the pope in the primacy of Peter as a permanent characteristic of the true Church.[17]

While the proof from the notes has largely been abandoned in Catholic literature, the *via primatus* is still being used in some of the apologetical treatises. Yet even if the historical basis of the

118

argument were stronger, it would be quite inadequate and, in fact, misleading. The visible mark of the true Church, according to this argument, is the Petrine tradition. The Catholic Church is the rightful heir of the apostolic Church because she possesses the Petrine heritage. But making papal primacy the distinguishing mark of the Church attributes to it a centrality in the life of the Church which it does not have. Catholics regard papal primacy along with episcopal collegiality as central in the institutional structure of the Church; but Catholics do not regard papal primacy as central in the Christian life as a whole. Central are the self-revelation of God in Christ and the communication in the Holy Spirit. Central are faith, hope, and love. Central is the presence of Jesus in the sacramental liturgy of the Church. According to Catholic teaching, the hierarchy is an essential part of the Church; but it is not primary, it is ministerial. It does not belong to the order of ends, but of means. The hierarchy, including papal primacy, is a service to the mystery of redemption present in the entire community and involving every one of the faithful. In other words, there are many divine gifts to the Church which are more central than papal primacy. Even a perfect historical proof of papal primacy as a gift of Christ— which is hardly available—would only deal with one of the ministerial gifts, and since these are subordinated to more important gifts, the proof would not show that the Catholic Church is the community of the faithful, in continuity with the New Testament, in which all the promises of Jesus are being fulfilled. To my mind, the apologetical argument based on papal primacy is misleading. It could suggest to Catholics and other Christians that the papal office is the great, central, Spirit-created reality in the Church's life. Such a view would falsify beyond recognition the picture of the Catholic Church. Such a view would foster a legalistic misunderstanding of the Catholic Church. The great, central Spirit-created reality in the Catholic Church is—as it is in all Christian Churches—the new life communicated to men.

We conclude that the traditional arguments—the *via historica, the via notarum,* even in its specialized form of the *via primatus* —attempting to prove the credibility of the Catholic Church are inadequate. That is to say, even on the assumption that the 19th-century notion of credibility is still useful, the proofs are not acceptable according to the historical and theological understanding of the contemporary Catholic theologian.

Why, then, are Christians Catholic? Does it make sense to be a Catholic? Has the claim of the Catholic Church become meaningless in the present? These are the questions which Charles Davis addresses to Catholic theologians. These are the kind of questions which the Catholic people, whether they be theologians or not, ask themselves in these days of doctrinal and institutional developments and the upheavals sometimes associated with them.

4.

The Credibility of the Church Today

IN our first chapter we defined the ecclesial mystery as the presence of God to sinful men, enabling them to become community. The mystery of Christ manifests itself wherever people, through God's presence to them, are reconciled to one another and thus become more truly themselves. This mystery is announced and celebrated in the Christian Church. While this redemptive mystery is operative everywhere, the message of this mystery and man's declared faith in it, are found only in the Christian Church or, more correctly, constitutes the Church in her being. Through the celebration of Word and sacrament and the presence of the Spirit, the Christian Church comes into being as the fellowship, local and universal, of the faithful. Despite the sinfulness that pervades the life of the Church and manifestations of social pathologies, the Church remains Church: in the power of the Spirit she continues to believe, proclaim, and celebrate the Good News, that is to say, the message of God's redemptive involvement in human life. The Church is constituted by a mystery that is, strictly speaking, universal.

In Chapter 1 we also acknowledged the presence of Christ in

all the Christian Churches. All the Churches are abodes of the Spirit. We acknowledge, moreover, that in the present day each Church is in need of dialogue and cooperation with the other Churches, and we expressed the hope that the ecumenical movement may eventually initiate the Churches into the identical self-understanding. We indicated also that today the unity and well-being of the Church demands dialogue and cooperation with the entire world of men; only in this way can the Church open herself unreservedly to God's redemptive presence in humanity. We have called this the Open Church.

The Catholic Claim

At the same time the Vatican Council continues to claim that among the Christian Churches, the Catholic Church holds a unique position.[1] There is a sense in which she is the one Church of the Lord. This special claim does not mean that Catholics are better Christians than others or that the Catholic Church is holier than other Churches. The claim has to do with the Catholic Church as an institution.

Some Catholics find this claim to uniqueness difficult to accept. They regard it as a remnant of institutional pride. They rejoice that at Vatican II the Catholic Church has understood herself as the Open Church, that is, that she has become sensitive to the redemptive work of God in other Churches and beyond them in the world of men; but they regard the continued insistence on Catholic uniqueness as an inconsistency and an unreasonable attachment to the past. Rosemary Ruether is an eloquent exponent of this view. Here is her way of formulating it: "Catholicism (in terms of its present, official statements)

122

operates out of a set of premises that, although showing progress
in ecumenical attitudes, nevertheless prevent it from being fully
ecumenical. Catholicism views itself as the place where the
Christian faith and the Church of Christ exist in their fullness.
It is in the fullest sense of the word 'the Church', i.e. the place
where Christ's work of redemption is in its most complete form.
. . . This model of understanding the Church makes it necessary
in some way or other (however this may be underplayed for
apologetical purposes) to define all other Christian traditions as
relatively inferior in relation to Catholicism. . . . I do not buy
this model. I do not regard Protestants as second-class Christians,
and I do not judge their faith relative to the Catholic model.
From the viewpoint of the previous model of Roman Catholicism, I am not a Roman Catholic."[2]

But from the viewpoint of another model Rosemary Ruether
does call herself Roman Catholic. She rejects the Protestant
model of the Church. In other words she does not acknowledge
that the 16th-century Reformers had the special insight into the
biblical message which gives the Churches of the Reformation
a privileged hold on the Gospel of Christ and makes them auto-
matically bearers of light and prophetic voices of reform. She
believes, rather, that the time has come when Catholics and
Protestants must abandon their exclusivist positions. Today
Christians are called to live the Christian life in a new age
where they must discover the meaning of Church and determine
new organizational forms of mutuality and social cohesion. "I
believe", she writes, "that we are called to be Christians first of
all, and not Protestants and Catholics, and that the terms 'Protestant' and 'Roman Catholic' should be regarded as statements of
our tribal affinity and responsibility and a confession of our sins,
and not statements of faith."[3] In this sense, then, in terms of

123

spiritual culture, liturgical experience and social heritage, Rosemary Ruether regards herself a Catholic.

Rosemary Ruether and Charles Davis hold positions that from one point of view are quite similar. Both reject the Catholic claim to uniqueness. At the same time, they differ widely on what this rejection implies. Charles Davis left the Catholic Church. It is his intention, moreover, to produce a set of arguments of public validity which shows that leaving the Catholic Church is the right thing to do. Rosemary Ruether, on the contrary, remains in the Catholic Church. She wishes to present arguments of public validity why Catholics who can no longer accept the traditional claim to uniqueness should continue to live, work, and pray in the Catholic Church. "One returns to the task of working amid the timebound and finite framework of the historical church institution, but only because one no longer takes them for the ultimate truth."[4] In this manner, each in his own Church, Christians are to work for renewal and the coming to be of the one Church in the present age.

The position of Rosemary Ruether is not unattractive. It appeals to something in the present-day experience of the Gospel. Any claim to uniqueness seems to prevent us from being open to the future. By regarding any truth as definitive we seem to close ourselves to the truth that is to come. A claim to uniqueness seems to make men defensive; instead of listening to the truth that God continues to speak in the experience of mankind, they have to find arguments to defend their positions. In the past, people have rejected the claim to uniqueness because of a relativism in regard to truth; today the people who reject this claim may not be relativists at all. They may believe in absolute truth, but they think that this truth is available in the contemporary answer to God's call in the present.

I think, nonetheless, that Rosemary Ruether's position is wrong. I do not follow her argument, first of all, because it does not give an account of the self-understanding of the Catholic Church today. Despite the extraordinary doctrinal development that has taken place, the Catholic Church at Vatican II still regards herself as the Church in a unique sense. Secondly, it seems to me that the people who advocate the emergence of a future Church, in discontinuity with the present Churches, operate out of a set of presuppositions, often quite unavowed, by which they evaluate theological positions and ecclesiastical developments as progressive or regressive: such a set of presuppositions, when clearly spelled out, constitutes, in fact, ecclesiological principles that lay claim to uniqueness. Hence the protest against uniqueness is more apparent than real.

In this chapter, therefore, I wish to deal with the Catholic Church's claim to uniqueness. According to Vatican II, this claim is still an essential part of the Church's self-understanding in faith. I wish to deal with the credibility of the Catholic Church's self-understanding in the present ecumenical age.

In Chapter 3 we saw that in the last century the word "credibility" acquired a special meaning. The credibility of Christian truth lay in the demonstration, based on historical records and the miracles reported in them, that this truth is of divine origin. While the truth itself could only be acknowledged by the gratuitous gift of faith—so the theory went—its credibility was rationally demonstrable. This radical distinction between faith and credibility has been largely abandoned.

The credibility I deal with in this chapter is understood in quite different terms. One may wonder, in fact, whether it is useful to retain the word "credibility" at all. The word is valuable, in my opinion, because it reminds us that we cannot escape the apologetical issue. We still have to ask the question why we believe. We have mentioned before that no insistence on the gracious and gratuitous character of Christian faith can ever dispense us from asking about the human reasons for believing. Faith inserts itself into human life; despite its divine character it is a dimension of human existence; we cannot escape the question about the human "why" of believing. There are some Protestant theologians who do not acknowledge the apologetical question. This question, they feel, seeks to subject the Word of God to human criteria. Their objection is, perhaps, more semantic than real, for even these Protestant theologians claim that faith is different from fanaticism, superstition, and schizophrenia and would be willing to render an account of these differences in terms of rational human experience. But this is the apologetical issue! What are the human reasons why men become and stay Christians? This is what I mean by credibility.

To clarify my understanding of credibility in this chapter, I wish to contrast contemporary apologetical inquiry—as I see it—with the apologetics created in the 19th century and traditional until recently.

First, apologetics is an inquiry within faith. The question is raised by the believer. It presupposes faith and the life of faith. It cannot be separated from this faith as an independent study. The study may inquire, for instance, whether there are urgent questions in human life to which faith gives an answer or whether there are human predicaments on which faith sheds some light. The study wants to give an account of the human reasons for believing and hopes to present these reasons in a language understandable to other people; yet this study in no way supposes that credibility can be rationally demonstrated by a set of arguments that have validity for non-believers. Apologetics deals with the questions which the believer asks about his own faith. Why do we believe? Does faith make sense?

From this follows a second characteristic. Apologetics addresses itself to Christians. It is not a search for rational arguments that will convince the non-believer of the rational foundation of the Christian faith. Apologetical reflection takes place within faith. Christians try to understand and formulate to themselves why they believe. The critical reason to which they submit their faith is their own. Why am I a believer? Is faith an escape, an infantile superstition? Or is it a dimension of life that opens men to reality and enables them to assume greater responsibility for themselves? In this context the objective, historical basis of the Christian creed must be examined. Ultimately, however, apologetics deals with the meaning of faith to the believer.

This leads to a third characteristic. Present-day apologetics, it seems to me, presupposes God's redemptive presence in human life. Apologetics replies to the question, "Does it make sense to believe?" We realize at once that faith cannot possibly make sense to man's sinful self. To man caught in the prison of his dividedness the Christian message has no meaning. To him it is a threat. To him it makes non-sense. But since God has involved himself in human life and since, therefore, the aspirations and questions of men are never simply their own effort to escape the human predicament but partly already realizations of a dialogue of salvation with God, the Gospel may indeed make sense to men. The question of credibility, therefore, presupposes the mystery of redemption revealed in Christ and present wherever people are.

The fourth characteristic is related to the third. The credibility of the Christian faith is meaningful to the non-Christian and hence has a certain public validity. Because the Christian believes in God's redemptive presence to all men, he is convinced that the reflections that make his faith credible to him will make sense to the non-Christian as well, even if he does not become a believer. The Christian does not plan his reflections for the non-believer; in apologetics he deals with a question that arises in his own life of faith. But he is carried by the conviction that the arguments of credibility will be meaningful also to others and, hence, that his faith will appear to the public as a reasonable kind of personal option.[5]

We cannot deal with the whole apologetical question here. We cannot study the questions "Why do people believe in God?" and "Why do people believe in Christ?" and "Why do people believe in the Church?" We single out a small question that fits into this chapter. "Why are Catholics Catholic?" or "Does the Catholic claim to uniqueness make sense? or "What is the credibility of the Catholic Church today?"

In keeping with the characteristics described above, I insist that this study of credibility is addressed to Catholics. It is not an attempt to find arguments persuading Protestants to join the Church of Rome. There are many good reasons for being Protestant. I do not see how a Catholic of the post-conciliar Church can still desire the conversion of Protestants to Roman Catholicism. What we desire for our Protestant fellow-Christians is what we desire for ourselves: that they live more deeply from the Gospel and participate in the renewal of their Church so that all the Churches come closer together in the common obedience to Christ. When I examine the credibility of the Catholic claim to uniqueness, I deal with a question posed by Catholics about their own faith.

Without attempting to justify my view in a wider study of apologetics, I define the credibility of the Catholic Church, especially of her claim to uniqueness, as the sense which the Church makes in terms of faith and experience. I will regard the Catholic Church as credible if its claim to be the one Church is meaningful in the terms of the New Testament, if it explains the past and if it illuminates the present.

THE TENSION BETWEEN LOCAL AND UNIVERSAL UNITY

The Gospel of Christ is God's gift to men. It is not a system of thought. It is not an organization. It is a living voice revealing the meaning of existence. The Gospel gives rise to action. The Gospel moves men to faith, to hope, and to love. There are tensions implicit in the gift of Christ, with which Christians must wrestle, and wrestling with them become open to the Spirit and be led on the way of life. I wish to show that the Catholic Church is meaningful in terms of the New Testament by describing the way in which she wrestles with two of these tensions and makes them sources of her ecclesiastical life. The first of these tensions is between local and universal unity.

Jesus Christ is the reconciler of men. His grace creates fellowship. There is in the Gospel a tension between the local and the universal aspect of the new community created by the presence of Christ. On the one hand we learn from the Scriptures that Jesus delivers man from his sin and enables him to love his neighbour. Christian faith opens a man to his fellows and initiates him into a new community. The books of the New Testament attribute central importance to the fellowship created by faith in Christ. The local congregation is the new family. In the writings of Paul words such as "*ecclesia*" and "*koinonia*" are used, first of all, as referring to the local congregation. Through the celebration of worship, especially the eucharist, the members of the congregation are brought into the fellowship of which Christ is source and centre. In this perspective the eucharistic meal, the participation in the same joyful supper, becomes the great sign revealing the nature of the new Christian community. Through Jesus, people become friends.

Equally central is the supplementary teaching that Jesus Christ is the saviour of mankind. Christ has come to deliver the human family from the powers of darkness that create hostility among them. Jesus is the messiah introducing a new age. He is the one mediator between God and man and, hence, the universal reconciler of people to their God and to one another. The books of the New Testament stress that Christ creates a fellowship that is universal. The community of the old covenant included only a single people; the new community convoked by Christ is all-inclusive, it embraces all nations. When the early Church proclaimed that in Christ the barrier between Jew and Gentile had been overcome, she announced the universality of Christ and the creation of a new community in which the differences between man and man are overcome and people are able to be themselves in the unity of faith and love. This community is, ultimately, identical with the human race. The act of God in Jesus Christ reveals the unity of the entire human family.

Christ's work of reconciliation, then, has two distinct aspects, the local and the universal. While there is a tension between them, they are inseparable. There may be times when it is more important to stress Christ's power to create fellowship among men and others when the main emphasis should be on Christ as saviour of a single people. The two aspects must never be separated. The tension between them, implicit in the Gospel, must be preserved. If either pole of the tension is abandoned, the unity which Christ brings is severely damaged. It is my contention that the Catholic Church, thanks to the Spirit, has always acknowledged this tension.

Today, thanks to the Spirit, the tension between the local and the universal is also acknowledged by the Churches associated with the ecumenical movement. For many of them this represents a recovery of a neglected aspect of the Gospel. Through the World Council of Churches many Protestant Churches express their faith in the universality of Christ's gift. In some of the union conversations between Churches, for instance in the Consultation on Church Union in the United States, the tension between the local and the universal is again understood as one of the central aspects of the reconciliation brought by Christ.

At an unusual evening session at the Faith and Order Conference, Montreal 1963, the issue of unity, local and universal, was raised by two biblical scholars.[6] The well-known Protestant exegete Ernst Käsemann challenged the idea that Jesus had come to create a universal unity among men. Unity, in its universal sense, is an eschatological concept. Käsemann tried to show that the notion of Church in the New Testament is so varied and the understanding of what Christ has done so diverse, that the historian has no good reason to speak of a single and universal Church in the New Testament. What we find in the Scriptures is the creation of local communities. The faith of these communities in the one Church expresses their hope in the age to come. The Catholic exegete Raymond Brown defended a contrary viewpoint. While he was willing to acknowledge the great diversity in the New Testament in regard both to the understanding of the Gospel and the notion of the Church, he thought there was good evidence in the Scriptures for asserting that the early Christians, in whatever local congregation, acknowledged the community created by Christ as one and universal. In attempting to spell out the relation of the new covenant to God's gifts under the old, the early Christians, in whatever community, affirmed the unity of the new people. The Churches of Christ were the Israel of God. In different images and analogies, the biblical writers interpreted the Church as the continuation of God's people on the threshold of history. This was, for instance, the deepest meaning of speaking of the Twelve. The unity of the twelve tribes in the covenant was carried forward in the unity of the many congregations in the new covenant. The Pauline epistles which speak of *ecclesia* and *koinonia* as synonyms for the local congregation, also describe the worship of these congregations—baptism and eucharist—in terms that recall the saving events of Israel's exodus and hence acknowledge the unity of the people. While the New Testament reveals various ecclesiologies and enables scholars to present these by laying stress on their differences, the New Testament also reveals the faith of these Christians, in whatever congregation, that they were the one people of God, in whom the ancient promises were fulfilled.

The discussion at the Montreal Faith and Order Conference brought out in dramatic fashion the tension, deeply inscribed in the Gospel of Christ, between the local and the universal understanding of Church. We cannot speak of the reconciliation brought by Christ without acknowledging the contrasting trends in the understanding of Church, as the few who enter into fellowship and become friends and as the many who participate in the same gifts and symbolize the unity which is the destiny of the whole human race.

The Catholic Church, I think, has never abandoned the tension between the local and the universal. In her own self-understanding the Catholic Church sees herself as the Church, one

and catholic, of which the creed speaks. She regards herself as a
body of local Churches—episcopally governed local Churches—
and at the same time as a single and world-wide people achiev-
ing visible unity through the papacy. In her own inner life the
Catholic Church has faced up to and wrestled with the tension
implicit in the New Testament. She has often been inefficient,
slow to adapt herself, overly inclined to compromise, too emphatic on authority . . . in brief, she has often suffered in her
life as Church because she would not give up the tension implicit in the Gospel. Other Christian Churches, it seems to me,
have abandoned the tension between the local and the universal.
They have regarded the health of the congregation and local
unity as paramount and hence have been willing to sacrifice the
unity of the universal community. They have abandoned one
pole of the tension. In their own self-understanding they did not
see themselves any more as the Church, one and catholic, of
which the creed speaks. Considering themselves as a part of the
Church they were unwilling or unable to live out the painful
tension between the local and the universal in their daily action
in the world. As an outsider looking upon the Orthodox
Churches it seems to me that even they have ceased to regard
themselves as the Church willing to live out, with its complica-
tions and its grandeur, the tension implicit in Christ's gift of
unity. It is through the ecumenical movement that these
Churches again take upon themselves the burden of this tension
and that the Catholic Church experiences this tension in a new
way.

Someone may suggest that the Catholic Church has abandoned
the tension by suppressing local unity. The Catholic Church, the
objection may run, has forgotten about the fellowship produced
by Christ in each place: the local community has been sacrificed

to universal unity. The Catholic Church, the objection may insist, has regarded the local Church simply as an administrative unit within the larger body of the Church. By abandoning the local in favour of the universal, the Catholic Church has become a monarchy.

There is some truth in this objection. The ecclesiastical tradition of the Roman Church has, for historical reasons, greatly stressed the universal Church and the supreme position and central role of the papacy. This stress has often restricted the life of the local Churches. We read of instances where it has crushed the creativity of local fellowships within the Church. The accusation that the Catholic Church has often forgotten the unity created by Christ among the few is therefore valid—but only up to a point. For despite the centralizing tendency of the papacy, the episcopal structure has always been retained in the Catholic Church. The presence of bishops announced the unity of the local Church and prevented the Catholic Church from abandoning the Gospel tension between the local and the universal. In other words, the social dynamics generated through the tension between episcopacy and papacy assure the presence of the Spirit that calls the Church out of the social pathologies constantly threatening it.

This tension is inscribed into the very structure of the Church. Episcopacy affirms the unity and relative autonomy of the local community and the papacy affirms the unity of the universal Church, in which the local communities participate. Even the First Vatican Council, in defining the supreme jurisdiction of the papacy, acknowledged and respected the episcopal structure of the Church: "This power of the pope is far from standing in the way of the power of ordinary and immediate episcopal jurisdiction by which the bishops who, appointed by the Holy Spirit in apostolic succession, feed and govern as true shepherds the particular flock assigned to them."[7] Even at Vatican I papal primacy was not understood in strictly monarchical terms. The other pole of the tension was acknowledged. The official explanations presented to the bishops at Vatican I specified the limitations of papal power.[8] They clearly indicate that the pope cannot dispense with the episcopal structure of the Church and that he cannot use his supreme authority to interfere in the ordinary and immediate episcopal government. The pope is to use his supreme power in the local Churches to build up and strengthen the Church universal or to help other bishops in exercising the governing function which is properly theirs.

The tension between the local and the universal was brought out more clearly at Vatican II. The key notion in this context is "collegiality". The Council taught that the bishops of the Catholic Church, together with the pope and under him, form a single body which, as such, is in apostolic succession. Collegiality means that a bishop is not simply the ruler and teacher of his own local Church but that, as a member of the college, he is also co-responsible for the policy-making and teaching of the Church universal. The bishops as a whole, therefore, share with the pope in the exercise of the highest ecclesiastical authority. Vatican II acknowledges a dialogue structure in the exercise of authority on the highest level and, in fact, on every level in the Church. According to the present understanding, laid down in the conciliar documents and echoing the teaching of Vatican I, the pope is free to teach and act in canonical independence from the bishops. His supreme jurisdiction, in the present understanding, is not derived from that of the bishops. At the same time, Vatican II has depicted the pope as head of the episcopal college and, hence, as acting in the name and on behalf of his brothers in the episcopate, even when he acts in canonical independence from them. In other words, Vatican II has provided doctrinal principles that enable the theologian to spell out the moral limits of papal authority.

What is, perhaps, more important is that Vatican II has re-discovered a better theological understanding of the local Church. It has acknowledged the creativity of the regional Churches. It has endorsed liturgical, legal, and theological pluralism within the Catholic Church.[9] It has provided a theology of decentraliza-tion. Thanks to the doctrinal and institutional evolution of Vatican II, the Gospel tension between the local and the uni-versal has become more central in the life of the Church. The living-out of this tension assures the presence of the Spirit.

Tension is not a peaceful word. Tension means discussion, dis-agreement, conflict, opposing tendencies. The stability of a com-munity in which tensions are alive lies in a dynamic balance to which all members contribute by their creativity as well as by their self-discipline. Thanks to the tension between the local and universal, enscribed in her collegial structure, the Catholic Church is able to come to consensus on the meaning of her own life of faith, which is acknowledged as authoritative by the faithful. Because of the complex interrelation between the re-gional Churches and the Church universal, between Churches in one area and Churches in another, between pope and bishops, between bishops, clergy and people, . . . the Catholic Church is able to enter into dialogue and even controversy on the mean-ing of her faith, discuss the problems on increasingly higher levels of authority, initiate the people into new issues and eventu-ally come to a definitive judgment, through pope and council, in which the entire Church has in some way participated and which all members are willing to regard as an authoritative expression of the Church's self-understanding.

The claim of the Catholic Church that, despite many pathological manifestations, it is capable of a doctrinal consensus is not an abstraction. We have experienced it at Vatican II. In Chapter 1 we have given one example of the doctrinal evolution that has taken place at Vatican II. It would be possible to study the social process which has led to this evolution and has eventually, after the complex back-and-forth of dialogue and even conflict, brought about the new doctrinal formulation. The present generation has experienced the Catholic Church as capable of expressing her self-understanding in a doctrinal consensus.[10]

The other Christian Churches, by abandoning the tension between the local and the universal, have lost the power of producing a consensus on the meaning of the faith acknowledged by their members. In the present union conversations the Christian Churches are trying to regain the authority to produce an agreement on what the Gospel means to them, in which all participate and which all regard as normative. At this time doctrinal consensus is unique in the Catholic Church. On this basis the Catholic Church must make a special contribution to the ecumenical movement.

I wish to be permitted a slight digression on the role of authority in the Church. In the perspective of the above reflections, authority appears as a precious gift to the Church. It is authority that enables the Church, in whom the Spirit produces understanding, to come to a consensus accepted by all. It is authority that enables the Church, vivified by the Spirit, to undergo corporate renewal. There are many reasons why Catholics in recent years have become highly critical of ecclesiastical authority. It is often true that hierarchy and people live in different worlds, that they have different problems and experience the Gospel in different terms. It is hard to find a cultural distance in the Western world as wide as that between an ordinary Christian in his environment and the highly artificial, courtly world of the Vatican. The basic experience of reality is so different between modern men in secular life and the princes of the Church in their Renaissance environment that it is unlikely that they will ask the same sort of questions about human life and human society. This is a dangerous situation. The present cultural separation between Catholics and the princes of the Church—symbolized perfectly by the clothes these men choose to wear—could undermine one of the great gifts the Church has received, namely her ecclesiastical authority.

Bernard McCabe, in a note in *New Blackfriars,* has analysed the present problem of authority in the Church in an instructive manner.[11] He distinguishes between pedagogical and representative authority. Pedagogical authority is exercised over others by a person who enjoys greater maturity, has access to more information, and has gone through a longer period of training. A teacher in a school exercises pedagogical authority. In terms of certain human perfections, such as wisdom, insight, experience, and skill, such a person is superior to his subjects. He has access to more truth, and hence it is right and reasonable to obey him. Representative authority, on the other hand, is exercised by a person who lays no claim to greater maturity or greater wisdom than other members of the community. His sources of information are largely available to the public. His skill may not be superior to that of others. He regards his subjects as his equals. Representative authority is exercised over others by a person who is able to formulate the common aspirations of the community. If the man appointed to authority is in touch with his community, through direct conversation and special institutions, then he is able to put into words and express, as practical policies, the common convictions and ideals of the people for whom he is responsible. He is able to formulate the demands of the common good, and hence it is right and reasonable to obey him. If authority is exercised in representative fashion, obedience enables people to identify more deeply with their community.

Bernard McCabe suggests that in the past the ecclesistical government understood its power as pedagogical authority. The Christian people acknowledged that popes and bishops had made great strides in the Christian life, that they had a special knowledge of the Scriptures, that they had a better grasp of Christian teaching, and that they had access to information not publicly available. There was a time when the people looked upon all governments in this way. What is happening today, Bernard McCabe suggests, is the transition from pedagogical to representative authority in the Catholic Church. Today no one believes any more that popes and bishops are more advanced in holiness than other Christians, or that they know the Scriptures better, or that they have access to secret information. Today popes and bishops are beginning to realize that they cannot exercise their authority unless they are in touch with the entire Church, through direct conversation and special institutions. Only through consultation and feedback do they become capable of formulating the aspirations the Spirit produces among the people and of making laws for the promotion of the new life which the Spirit creates in the community. The Christian who obeys the ecclesiastical authority in this situation serves the common good of the entire community.

The transition from pedagogical to representative authority is uneven in the Church. This is the reason for the crisis of authority! There are superiors who still understand their authority as pedagogical while their people have assimilated a sense of representative authority. Conversely, there are people who desire to be ruled by pedagogical authority—they yearn for superiors who treat them as pupils—while they may, in fact, live under ecclesiastical superiors who exercise representative authority and refuse to treat their people as minors. While the transition is uneven, it is inevitable. The social process—such as dialogue and consultation—created by Vatican II changes the self-understanding of Christians in the Church.

Is this representative authority in keeping with Catholic teaching? This question must be asked. In recent years Pope Paul has repeatedly rejected a new understanding of authority that regards the superior simply as the recorder of public opinion. Pope Paul VI has reproved the attempt to limit the role of authority to registering and expressing the opinions found among the people.[12] The Pope rightly insists that such an understanding would be the undoing of the authority Christ gave to the Church.

Yet what we have called representative authority is in keeping with Catholic teaching. According to this understanding of authority the superior records and *evaluates* the opinions found among his people. Dialogue, through direct conversation and special institutions, enables him to be in touch with the ideals and aspirations of his community, but what counts most in his eyes is whether the convictions are close to the Gospel of Christ, whether they are creative responses to the questions asked in the Church, whether they are simply repetitions of traditional phrases or ideas that have emerged in dialogue and reflection. The ecclesiastical superior, in other words, listens to the Spirit speaking in the community. He tests the convictions of men with the Gospel. He is willing to let himself be addressed by God's Word present in the experience of his people. Superiors exercising representative authority are open to all the opinions in the Church, but by an act that is properly creative, and not simply by recording majority views, they try to formulate the convictions the Spirit is producing in the community and to detect the direction in which the Church is being moved by this Spirit.

These reflections on the crisis of authority today show that what is happening in the Church, the changes, the new life, the experiments, even the turmoil and the uncertainties, are signs that the Catholic Church is becoming more truly a community in dialogue and that she submits more faithfully to the Gospel tension between the local and the universal. The true meaning of the present period of transition will emerge more clearly in the following section.

THE TENSION BETWEEN PAST AND PRESENT

We now wish to examine another tension implicit in the Gospel of Christ. Implicit in God's gift of himself in Jesus Christ is a tension between past and present. On the one hand, we believe that everything God has done for the salvation of man has happened in Jesus Christ and hence lies in the past, and on the other, we believe that the divine work of redemption, revealed in Christ, is still going on and hence is present to us. Redemption happened in the life, death, and resurrection of Jesus; and redemption is still happening in the present, freeing men to enter into their future. Redemption took place once and for all in the past; and yet it is forever contemporary to us. This is the tension between past and present.

The two poles of this tension belong to the core of Christian proclamation. We affirm categorically that in Jesus Christ God has acted on behalf of the entire human family. In him the sins of the human race have been forgiven, in him all men are reconciled to the Father, in him the entire future of the human family is contained. Scripture and tradition affirm that in Christ God has revealed himself in a definitive way. In Christ God has communicated himself to men as saviour once and for all. Because the apostles give witness to this definitive event, we call their witness normative for the life of the entire Church. Because God has done everything for the salvation of men in Jesus Christ, nothing can be added to the apostolic witness by which he is present to us. The Church has proclaimed this once-for-all character of God's gift in Christ from the very beginning. Already in the New Testament we read the appeal "to contend for the faith once for all delivered to the saints".[13]

At the same time, however, Christ is present to men in the Spirit. The life, death, and resurrection of Christ are realities to which the believer has access now. God continues to communicate himself in them to the Christian Church. They are contemporary to the believer. What Jesus did to men when he lived on earth, when he taught, when he suffered, died, and rose, he continues to do to people in the Church who participate in the sacramental liturgy in which the paschal mystery is present to them. The self-communication of God in Christ continues in the Church. In Christ God gives himself to us in the present so that we may be able to choose our future. Here, then, are the terms of the tensions: divine redemption took place "once for all" and yet it is "forever present".

To be faithful to the Gospel the Church must hold on to the two poles of this tension. She must defend the once-for-all character of redemption and, at the same time, proclaim its present reality. The Church must express and communicate the redemptive mystery as ever present and yet as self-identical with the redemption that took place in Jesus Christ many centuries ago.

What happens in the Church when this tension is abandoned? If the present is abandoned in favor of the past, then the original apostolic community becomes, in a literal sense, the model of present-day church life. The biblical record becomes the one locus of divine revelation, to which the Church must refer herself in her preaching and to which the Christian must turn in his faith. To be in touch with the Christ-event would then always mean to return to the past, to the record of the past, to the language and thought-forms of the past. To abandon the tension between past and present by forgetting God's present self-revelation, leads to some form of primitivism.

Some primitivism exists in every Church. Certain Protestant notions of the written Word appear to the Catholic as a kind of primitivism. The Good News is regarded as codified once for all in the New Testament: the preaching of the Church, on this hypothesis, is simply the repetition of the apostolic preaching. The message of the Church today is simply the reiteration of the original message preached two thousand years ago. The more faithful the Church becomes to biblical preaching and the more conformed in her structure to the apostolic community, the more open she is, on this hypothesis, to the Holy Spirit and the more powerful will be her saving influence.

This primitivist position does not only exist among fundamentalists. It is a wider phenomenon. It is found as a trend among sophisticated theologians in a variety of ways. The decision to regard any particular period of the Church's life as normative in the sense that it is worthy of repetitive imitation by the Church of a later age, abandons the tension implicit in the Gospel between past and present. A kind of primitivism is found, it seems to me, in many forms of Protestantism: the life of the early Christians, as understood through the great Reformers of the 16th century, is often regarded as a model for the life of the Church of later ages. Catholics are sometimes primitivists in regard to the 13th century: they think of renewal simply as a slight adaptation to modern life of a medievally patterned Church—as they might think of contemporary philosophy as an updating of Thomism. All Christians, of course, regard the apostolic witness recorded in the Scriptures as normative for the total life of the Church: but this does not imply that fidelity to this norm means repeating the doctrinal formulations of the New Testament or imitating the ecclesiastical structure of the early Church. The biblical and liturgical movements in the Catholic Church may have inspired some Catholic authors to suggest, in a mood of enthusiasm, that the more conformed the present Church is to the apostolic community, in teaching, worship, and ministry, the more faithful she is to the divine self-communication in Christ. But the call to "return to the Scriptures" or "return to the sources" need not advocate primitivism of any kind. For the Church, as we shall see, can be faithful to the apostolic witness only by being simultaneously faithful to God's self-identical Word addressed to her in the present.

The tension between past and present can also be abandoned at the other pole. It is possible to insist on the present action of the Spirit in the community of believers in such a way that the self-identity between present redemption and the event once for all revealed in Christ is being sacrificed. If the previous tendency is called primitivist, this tendency could be called modernist. Since God is at work among men today and since, therefore, the aspirations of men are, partially at least, fruits of the divine work in them, it may be tempting to insist on the presence of the divine action without seeking to establish whether what occurs in the Church today is identical with what happened in Jesus Christ at the beginning. Since the ultimate guarantee of God's work in the present is the conformity with the original gift, the indifference to the New Testament record and the witness of the early Church leads to religious confusion and the corruption of the divine gifts.

There is some modernism in all the Christian Churches. We certainly have had modernist authors in the Catholic Church. The theological systems produced by some Protestant thinkers of the 19th and 20th centuries clearly belong to this category. They wanted to present a view of the religion of Jesus or of the Gospel message that would be contemporary and correspond to the aspirations of the people, but because they moved away from the original gift, crystallized in the Scriptures, their views could not affirm themselves for long as authentic interpretations of divine revelation.

The tension between past and present is the crucial problem of all the Churches today. It seems to me that today all the Churches want to be faithful to the original apostolic witness, and at the same time express this Gospel in a contemporary manner. But are all the Churches capable of doing this? It seems to me that the Catholic Church, because of its concept of "tradition", is capable of retaining the two poles of this tension between past and present. The Catholic Church has defended the concept of tradition against the attempt of the 16th-century Protestants to present the Bible alone as the measure of truth. The Catholic Church has affirmed that the handing-on of the Gospel is a process in which the Spirit is creatively involved.

145

Tradition is not the passing-on of a book of biblical or creedal formulas; it is not a mechanical repetitive process by which that which was said in the past is uttered again in the present. It is a creative process in which the Gospel, once for all delivered to the saints, is stated and re-stated as God's Word for the age in which the Church lives. Because the Holy Spirit is involved in this process, the Catholic Church speaks of "divine tradition".

It seems to me that—apart from the Catholic Church—the Christian Churches that insist on conformity with the Gospel (and hence refuse to become modernist) are tied to a particular period of the past, to the New Testament record, or to the consensus of the first five centuries, or to the witness of the undivided ancient Church, or to the confessional documents of the 16th century. Even the Churches which profess an understanding of "divine tradition" and thereby affirm that God is present in their manner of proclaiming the Good News, have tied themselves to the documents of the past and no longer seem to have confidence that the Spirit who at one time enabled them to formulate the great creeds in a creative way, in harmony with the Scriptures and yet in response to contemporary problems, is any longer at work in the present process of handing on the Gospel. Only the Catholic Church has a teaching on divine tradition that she is willing to apply to the present. The Catholic Church believes that the process of formulating doctrine, which the Spirit produced in the past, continues to go on in the present. The divine tradition alive in the Church today has enabled the Catholic Church to reinterpret her doctrinal position at Vatican II and renders her capable of continuing this in the future.

This traditioning of the Gospel in the Church is often called "development of doctrine." It was, above all, the work of John Henry Newman, in his celebrated *Essay on the Development of*

Christian Doctrine, that assigned this creative concept of tradition its central place in the understanding of the Church. Development, for Newman, belongs to the very nature of an idea.[14] The truth reveals its total meaning only slowly as it is applied in different situations, challenged by opponents and made to explain various aspects of life, as it is made to reply to new questions, related to other insights and confronted with the manifold experience of mankind. Truth is fully assimilated through a process that is vital and communal. It includes the logical, the psychological, and the social. It is through the history in which an entire people is involved that a truth reveals the full depth of its meaning. The Gospel, then, according to Newman, reveals its rich meaning and its many aspects only through the history of the Church as it is alive in the faithful reflection of the community and responds to the questions of the ages. In the view of Newman, only the Church in which there is a perpetual development of doctrine is the community in which the Spirit provides the fullness of truth to the faithful. True Church, for Newman, is only the Catholic Church.

How did Newman preserve the tension between past and present? How can one be sure that the development of doctrine that has taken place in the Church is not a corruption but an authentic development preserving, strengthening, and deepening the original message? Are there tests whereby we may study the developments that have occurred, and still occur, in the life of the Christian Church and evaluate whether these are deformations of the revealed message or authentic developments bringing to light its latent content? In his *Essay* Newman gives seven such tests.[15] Authentic development of doctrine is assured if there is in the Church the preservation of its own type, the continuity of its own principles, the power of assimilation, logical

147

sequence, the anticipation of the future, the conserving action of its past, and finally its chronic vigour. In this way, according to Newman, the Church lives out the tension between past and present and hears the self-identical Word of God addressed to her in Christ, then and now.

Since the days of Cardinal Newman, the development of doctrine has become one of the principal subjects studied by Catholic theologians and historians. Many theories have been proposed to explain doctrinal development in the Church.[16] All theologians agree that divine revelation is closed with Jesus Christ and the witness to him by the apostles; all theologians agree that teachings proposed by the Church in later years, yet not explicitly found in the apostolic witness, are not new revelations. In some way they must have been contained in the original revelation or have been generated by it. Theories of doctrinal development want to show the complex process—charismatic, logical, psychological, experiential—by which new teaching has been drawn from the deposit of faith, once for all delivered to the saints. The authors of the 19th century and even the majority of authors of the 20th century have proposed theories of *homogeneous* doctrinal development. By homogeneous they meant the unbroken continuity between a new formulation of doctrine and the formulation that preceded it. Doctrinal development is called homogeneous when the new formulation is derived—logically, psychologically, or in some other way—from the preceding formulation so that it should be possible to trace an unbroken step-by-step process by which present teaching has been drawn from the original deposit of faith. It is in virtue of this homogeneity that Catholic theologians defended the doctrinal development in the Catholic Church as a faithful expression of the divine message revealed in Christ. According to them, it was because

148

of this Spirit-produced homogeneity or unbroken continuity that the Catholic Church today announces the self-identical Word of God.

In recent years Catholic theologians have expressed hesitations in regard to the various theories (including Newman's) of homogeneous development of doctrine.[17] The first reason for this hesitation is that it does not seem to explain the development of doctrine recorded in the New Testament. If we compare the teaching of various New Testament writers, for instance the christology of Mark, Luke, and John, we see a development; but there is no evidence for assuming that this development took place homogeneously. There is no evidence for thinking that previous formulations were known to the later writer and that his doctrinal positions were, in some manner, drawn from the previous formulations. It would appear, rather, that in the various parts of the early Church the apostolic teachers expressed the same Gospel in original ways—and hence differently—as responses, guided by the Spirit, to the questions and aspirations of their communities. Few biblical scholars today explain as homogeneous development the doctrinal evolution recorded in the books of the New Testament.

Catholic theologians have hesitations regarding the theories of homogeneous development also on other grounds. The various theories seem to presuppose a rather intellectualistic understanding of divine revelation. They tend to equate divine revelation with divine teaching: the revelation of God in Christ was present to the apostles mainly as a set of teachings. It is upon this original teaching, according to the theories of homogeneous development, that later generations reflected in new situations, with new questions and new insights, and formulated relevant doctrinal positions that were implications contained in the original message or necessary inferences drawn from it.

The Second Vatican Council, especially in the *Constitution on Divine Revelation,* presents a deeper understanding of divine revelation.[18] Revelation is God's self-communication to men in the experience of Israel and, finally and definitively, in Jesus Christ and the experience of the apostolic community. This divine revelation is recorded, under the influence of the Spirit, in the Scriptures. But this revelation cannot simply be equated with the apostolic testimony and the biblical literature which gives witness to it. The Word of God transcends every expression of it in the Church. The Word of God, moreover, is a living Word. Divine revelation is closed with the apostolic witness to Christ, in the sense that God has totally revealed himself in Christ and that, after Christ, no further self-revelation of God is possible. Jesus not only reveals the Word of God, he is this Word. To expect another revelation after Jesus would be a denial of his divinity. At the same time, divine revelation must be said to continue in the Church, in the sense that God keeps on saying in the Church what he said once and for all in Jesus Christ. The revelatory self-communication of God continues in the Church. The Word continues to address men and the Spirit continues to enable men to receive this Word in faith. Through the celebration of the liturgy, including Word and sacrament, and through the more invisible self-communication of God in the Spirit, the living Word continues to evoke the faith of the Christian Church and constitute it as the community of the faithful. The self-identical Gospel is continually revealed in the Church.

From this it follows that listening to the Gospel is not simply the Spirit-guided reflection on the teaching once for all revealed;

Christians listen to the self-revealing God addressing them through the Scriptures and the witness of the Church. The Church is faithful not simply to a set of truths revealed to her at the beginning; she is faithful to the living Word that comes to her in the present as the ever-identical Gospel. The theories of homogeneous doctrinal development seem to suppose that God has once revealed his message to men in Christ and that the on-going divine assistance in the Church is simply the Spirit aiding her in understanding more deeply the meaning of this message. However, a better understanding of revelation brings out that the self-disclosure of God is more deeply involved in the history of the Church and her contemporary faith. God has spoken once for all in Christ, in his teaching, his life, death, and resurrection; at the same time, God continues to utter the self-same Word through the proclamation of the apostolic witness and other more hidden ways in the Church. In her faith the Church acknowledges God's living Word in the original witness as well as the identical Word addressed to her, and constituting her, in the present. Will this deeper understanding of revelation in the Church affect what we mean by doctrinal development?

There is another reason why I have great hesitations in regard to the theories of homogeneous doctrinal development. The doctrinal development that has taken place at Vatican II can hardly be described as homogeneous. The development of certain doctrinal positions at Vatican II represent something like a quantum leap. We have studied one remarkable doctrinal shift in Chapter 1. At Vatican II we have passed from a restrictive to an open understanding of the Church. What has happened here was not the further penetration of the previous understanding of Church. The new understanding was not implicitly contained in the preceding one. The new teaching was a leap. It was well-founded, of course, in contemporary Catholic experience, in a new reading of the Scriptures, and in theological reflections that had, for many years, been the object of dialogue in the Church; yet it was a leap nonetheless. The idea of the Open Church provoked vehement opposition in the conciliar hall. In whatever context the open understanding of Church was expressed, in relation to other Christians, to Jews, to members of other religions, and to people in general, it created a most revealing controversy among the Council fathers. Many bishops felt that the new concept was in opposition to the previous one: the Open Church was a betrayal of the traditional, restrictive Church, confirmed by Pius XII. No set of logical arguments could convince the opponents of the new position that the Open Church was in perfect continuity with traditional teaching. It became clear that what was required in the transition from the old to the new position was a kind of conversion. The doctrinal development that took place at Vatican II was not a passage from the implicit to the explicit, but a new response to God's Word in a new age. With a new question in mind, the bishops listened to the Word of God, revealed in past and present, and in formulating its meaning they were willing to transcend the doctrine of the preconciliar Church. The doctrinal position adopted by Vatican II was not in unbroken continuity with the previous position, it was a re-interpretation of teaching in obedience to God's Word in the present.

To characterize this non-homogeneous development that took place at Vatican II I shall introduce a new term. I shall speak of a re-focusing of the Gospel. What do I mean by focus? Every age has its central questions; every age has its special way of seeing life; every age has its own way of being threatened and its own aspirations for a more human form of existence. In his

Towards an American Theology, Herbert Richardson has called this the "intellectus" of an age or culture.[19] Since the divine self-revelation in Christ is the Good News for every age, the same and identical message will be focalized differently in different ages, depending on the principal problems of men and their deep aspirations. The "intellectus" of an age—to use Richardson's vocabulary—influences the manner in which the Church proclaims the Gospel. God saves men from the dangers that lie hidden in their "intellectus" and reveals to them the redemptive possibilities present in them. In every age, therefore, the Gospel is proclaimed with a central message and thrust, which is the saving response of God to the self-questionings of men. This I call the focus of the Gospel.

The central message and thrust of the Gospel is the focal point, in relation to which the entire doctrine of salvation is proclaimed and understood. The entire teaching of the Church is grouped around this focus. All the doctrines which make up the Church's teaching assume meaning and reveal their significance through their connection with the focal point of the Gospel. As the Church enters a new spiritual-cultural environment in which people see life differently, have new questions and new ideals, she seeks to proclaim the Gospel with a new central message and thrust as the divine response to the central problems of the age. The new spiritual-cultural climate demands the re-focusing of the Gospel. Yet as the old focus gives way to the new, the entire doctrinal synthesis of the past falls apart in order to be made anew in the light of the new focus. The old way of seeing doctrines together in unity is dissolved: what is required in the new situation is their re-interpretation in the light of the new focal point. We hope to examine this more carefully in the following pages.

The non-homogeneous or discontinuous doctrinal development that took place at Vatican II—the doctrine of the Open Church—was a shift (or, at least, the beginning of a shift) in the focal point of the Gospel and demands, as I hope to show, a re-interpretation of the Church's teaching.

How is the self-identity of the Gospel preserved in discontinuous doctrinal development? We shall discuss this further on. For the moment I wish to mention that the recognition of different possible focal points in the proclamation of the Gospel enables us to account for the doctrinal differences in the books of the New Testament. Each author listened to God's Word in Christ from a particular view point, largely determined by the spiritual-cultural situation of the Christian community to which he belonged. Each author preached the Good News with the focus required for making it God's Word of salvation to his people. The several focal points in the books of the New Testament explain why it is impossible to reconcile the various positions into a single consistent system of thought.

We must examine more carefully what we mean by re-focusing the Gospel. We contend that there are moments in the history of the Church when her fidelity to the unchanging Gospel produces a doctrinal development that is discontinuous. This happens when the Church enters a new spiritual-cultural situation. To proclaim the Gospel in a manner comprehensible to her age, the Church must translate her message into the language and the concepts of the culture in which she lives and reply to the questions which are being asked in her day. This the Church wants to do not simply for the sake of outsiders to whom she preaches the Good News; she wants to do this for the sake of the Christian community itself. Her own members will come to think and speak in the manner learnt in their society, and if the Gospel

154

makes sense to them they will eventually think about it and speak about it in terms drawn from their spiritual-cultural experience of life. This need for "accommodated preaching" is acknowledged in the documents of Vatican II. It is called "the law of all evangelization". Here is the entire paragraph.

"Thanks to the experience of past ages, the progress of the sciences, and the treasures hidden in the various forms of human culture, the nature of man himself is more clearly revealed and new roads to truth are opened. These benefits profit the Church, too, for, from the beginning of her history, she has learned to express the message of Christ with the help of the ideas and terminology of various peoples, and has tried to clarify it with the wisdom of philosophers, too. Her purpose has been to adapt the Gospel to the grasp of all as well as to the needs of the learned, insofar as such was appropriate. Indeed, this accommodated preaching of the revealed Word ought to remain the law of all evangelization. For thus each nation develops the ability to express Christ's message in its own way. At the same time, a living exchange is fostered between the Church and the diverse cultures of people."[20]

The "accommodated preaching of the revealed Word" urged by Vatican II raises the main problem of the Church today. Most Catholics in our day agree that we are entering upon a new spiritual-cultural environment. This was certainly the evaluation of the present situation in the *Constitution on the Church in the Modern World*. There is need today to accommodate the preaching of the Gospel to the world in which we live. Yet in what does this accommodation consist?

Some Catholics seem to suggest that this process of translation is simply the retelling of the Good News in a new language and with the use of new concepts. They seem to suggest that the work to be done is mainly intellectual or philosophical. While the Catholic Church in the past used concepts derived from the classical philosophies—since the 13th century especially the thought of Aristotle—, the task of the Church in our times, it is said, is to translate the Christian creed into a new langauge and new concepts derived from the cultural environment in which we live. Yet, if the task of reformulating the Gospel is regarded as a philosophical undertaking, as an intellectual exercise in translation, then this Gospel is in grave danger of being conformed to the wisdom of men and of thus losing its power. Since the Gospel has been given us as a divine critique of the cultures in which we live, any attempt to translate it on a purely conceptual level threatens to falsify the divine message. Pope Paul VI has repeatedly warned of the dangers implicit in the attempt to adapt the Gospel to the culture in which we live.[21]

The point I wish to make here is that the "accommodated preaching of the revealed Word"—called "the law of all evangelization" by Vatican II—which is demanded of the Church as she enters a new spiritual-cultural environment is not simply a work of translation (and hence an intellectual exercise), but a work of re-focusing the Gospel (and hence a work of faith and in faith). The new cultural environment provides Christians not only with new language and new concepts in which to think; it also brings with it new problems, new preoccupations, new aspirations. For this reason I have always spoken of *spiritual*-cultural environments. The Church in such a situation must accommodate her preaching to reply to new questions and proclaim the Good News of salvation to people who experience the values of life in a new way. The task at hand is, therefore, the re-focusing of the Gospel. This process is not, first of all, an intellectual one. It is a process that challenges the faith and the faithfulness of the entire Christian community, a process of discernment, of new listening to God's Word, of finding, in faith, the meaning of the Gospel for the dilemmas and problems of the present generation. Here there is no danger of a cultural assimilation of the Gospel. For what is sought is not greater fidelity to the language and concepts of the present culture, but greater fidelity to the Word of God speaking to the Church in the present. The re-focusing of the Gospel preserves the tension between the past and the present: when the Church proclaims divine revelation as the Good News for the present generation, she is faithful to the Word once for all spoken in Christ and faithful to the self-same Word uttered in the Church now and constituting her being in the present.

Because of the Catholic acknowledgment of "divine tradition" that is, because of the Catholic teaching that in the process of handing on the Gospel the Spirit is creatively involved, the Catholic Church is able to re-focalize the Gospel in a new spiritual-cultural situation.

In the following pages I wish to examine more carefully the doctrinal development called the re-focusing of the Gospel. I shall base myself mainly on the doctrinal development that took place at Vatican II, in particular on the doctrinal shift, studied in Chapter 1, to the Open Church.

The first step in the re-focusing of the Gospel is the Church's discernment of the crucial problems proper to the culture in which she lives. What are the principal threats to human life, personal and social, in the culture in which the Gospel is to be Good News? The Church discerns the demonic in the present age. What are the enemies of human life in the contemporary world? Since Jesus is saviour and, as such, has come to save us from the enemies of life, the Church's understanding of present evil will help her to find the central message and thrust which the Gospel has for the present age.

The first task of the Church in a new spiritual-cultural environment is the discernment of the demonic. This discernment, I wish to insist, is already the work of the Spirit. Concern with the deep questions of life is already redemptive, for it delivers us from concern with superficial questions and makes us abandon preoccupations with what is unreal. The Spirit enables us to ask the right questions. This is true, I wish to add, for Christians and non-Christians alike. Part of us may reach out to recognize the deepest threat to our human existence, but because of the dividedness into which we are born there is another part in us that is afraid of the truth; this part of us makes us hide from the deep questions by attaching ourselves to pseudo-questions or by focusing on evil that is only peripheral. The Church herself is tempted to focus her attention on superficial evil in order to avoid facing the real threats to human and Christian existence. When men do face the central problems of life something has happened to them, of which they are not the sole authors. The Spirit of God has enabled them to leave their fears behind and discern the demonic that threatens human life, personal and social, in their day.

Vatican II has attempted to analyse the present spiritual-cultural situation of man today. *The Constitution on the Church in the Modern World* describes the cultural change that has taken place and characterizes the anguish and the hopes of the present generation. This is done, above all, in the celebrated Introductory Statement. In this Statement the Vatican Council acknowledges that at present the human race "is passing through a new stage in its history",[22] that the social and cultural transformation that is going on "has repercussions on man's religious life",[23] and that "today's spiritual agitation and the changing conditions of life are part of a broader and deeper revolution".[24] The Statement attempts to give a description of this transformation. It sums up its own description in the sentence, "The human race has passed from a rather static concept of reality to a more dynamic evolutionary one".[25] In this new context the Church seeks to discern the deepest anguish of man, his profound problems and the evil that threatens to undo his life.

The principal questions today are: Who are we? Who are we as persons? Who are we as people? Who are we as mankind? Man is threatened in his human existence, personal and social, by forces of disintegration.

In a previous chapter I have analysed the presence of evil in human life in terms of dividedness. This comes close to the preoccupation of the conciliar document. Since we have become a large family living on the limited territory of the earth, since modern means of communication and transportation have turned the earth into a small planet, and since the growing interdependence of social life has made people more dependent on one another, we experience the dividedness of the human race as the central threat against social life. The forces that pit man against man, nation against nation, class against class—many of them, as we have seen, pathological—have gained such power in the present cultural situation that they cause human misery of unprecedented proportions and may even provoke a catastrophe that could destroy human life altogether. This dividedness of human life is related to the dividedness in the heart of man, man's own self-alienation, the inherited sin into which we are born.

We now come to *the second step* in re-focusing the Gospel. After the Church has discerned the demonic and the principal

Word. Since there are many voices heard in the experience of the human community, the difficulty is to discern the Word of God in history. This is the task of the Church.

The Constitution on the Church in the Modern World is the first ecclesiastical document that clearly acknowledges the presence of God's Word in history and the Church's duty to listen to it. The technical expression used here is "the signs of the times".[26] God addresses the Christian Church through the signs of the times. We read: "The people of God believe that they are led by the Spirit of the Lord who fills the earth. Motivated by this faith, they labour to decipher the authentic signs of God's presence and purpose in the happenings, needs and desires in which they have part with the other men of our age. For faith throws a new light on everything, manifests God's design for man's total vocation and this directs the mind to solutions which are fully human".[27]

God addresses the Church in his Word through the Scriptures, through past tradition, and through present experience in the Church and the human community as a whole. In her attempt to be faithful to the living Word the Church must listen to the Gospel proclaimed in her as well as to the experience of men in the history of which she is part. Since God addresses the whole of mankind the Church must be in touch with the experience of the entire human family in order to become truly faithful to the Word of God. These considerations lead us to reiterate a conclusion of a previous chapter: the Church needs the world to become truly Church.

But how does the Christian discern the Word of God in history? Many voices make up the experience of society. How does the Christian know that the voice he hears is from God, and not the product of man's self-seeking? How does he know that by listening to history he is not being led into self-destruction and human pride? The Church, in the words of the conciliar document, "always has the duty to scrutinize the signs of the times and of interpreting them in the light of the Gospel".[28] The faith preached by the Church enables the Christian to discern the divine message in history. The Word of God present in Scripture and the life of the Church enables the Christian to sift the experience of society, and to detect whether the values, aspirations, and deep convictions of the present generation are produced by the Spirit and hence embody the Word of God, or whether they are the products of man's sinfulness—of his trend to assert himself against others or his capacity to use his intelligence to flee from the challenges of life.

The Christian moves from the Church into the world. Behind him he hears the Word of God celebrated in the believing community; and coming toward him, from the world which he enters, is the same Word of God present in the experience of history.[29] But the Word present in history comes to the Christian in a chorus made up of many voices. The Word of God, proclaimed in the Church, addressing him, as it were, from behind enables the Christian to discover in this chorus the Word of God present in history. This Word in history, being self-identical with the Word revealed in Christ, makes itself known to the Christian by the harmony and coherence with the biblical message. The Christian, formed by the preaching of the Church, will be able to detect in the experience of the world those values and convictions which have a correspondence and connaturality with the Gospel of Christ. In this process of listening to God speaking in the world, Christians may come to diverse views: some may hear God's voice in certain experiences of mankind and others may evaluate the same experiences quite differently. But through sustained dialogue and common action among Christians, the process of listening will be purified and corrected, and eventually converge toward a consensus of the believing community. The final assurance that God is speaking to us through the experience of mankind is given only when the entire Church, through an act of her teaching authority, assisted by the Spirit, acknowledges the presence of God's Word.

We must look more closely at this process of listening to God's Word speaking in history. As the Christian moves into the world and takes seriously, not only the questions of men but also their significant and precious experiences, he will constantly refer back to the Scriptures and the Church's teaching to test whether these experiences are in harmony or in discord with the divine revelation once for all delivered to the apostles. If the Christian has, in fact, been addressed by God's Word present in the world, then he will read the Scriptures and interpret the tradition with a new sensitivity. He may find biblical themes and doctrinal hints which escaped him before. He may be able to relate aspects of doctrine which before he was unable to connect. Listening to the divine Word in history may initiate him into a renewed understanding of the Gospel message. But the judgment that the experience of mankind and the scriptural message are in harmony and that, therefore, this experience is God's Word addressed to the Church is not scientifically or rationally demonstrable. The only assurance for this judgment is the experience of the Church. The final verdict belongs to the ecclesiastical magisterium.

We see here clearly the creative moment in the divine tradition of the Church. What goes on in the Church in the faithful traditioning of the Gospel in a changed environment is not a simple repetition of the primitive message, it is not even reducible to the primitive message by purely logical means; what is involved here is an indefinable moment, the work of the Spirit in the community, by which the Church judges that a certain experience in which she shares, coheres with the Gospel once for all received by the apostles, and hence gives witness to the self-same divine Word. As the Church listens to this divine Word present in history, she lays hold of the Gospel in a new way. The Word of God coming toward the Church from her encounter with history enables her to see her divine message from a new viewpoint as addressing itself to a new issue, and having a new central impact. And this is precisely what we have called the re-focusing of the Gospel.

I want to illustrate the second step in re-focusing the Gospel by analyzing the doctrinal shift from closed to open Church that took place at Vatican II. The Church discerned the demonic and the main threats to human existence in the divisiveness that pervades the lives of men and has reached an unprecedented climax in the present age. How is her message Good News in such an age? Taking this question to heart, the Church began to realize that the manner in which the Gospel was understood and presented in the past often added to the divisiveness in human life. Have Christians contributed more to the divisions among men than to their reconciliation? To a world already divided, we have added the difference between Christian and non-Christian, — understood in such a radical way that it became the source of countless divisions, strifes, injustices, and even wars. And have we not, as Christians, added to the world the division among the Churches? Is not the Catholic Church in some cultures of the West a source of divisiveness? Do we not gather Catholics from the rest of the population in separate societies and institutions? Is not the difference between Catholic and non-Catholic a strong emotional reality for the ordinary Catholic which makes him live in the world as a divider rather than a reconciler of man?

The *Constitution on the Church in the Modern World* deals with these questions as no authoritative text of the Christian tradition ever has. In a special chapter it explains that the Gospel is not a divisive reality but a reconciling factor in the world.[30] The gifts of the Gospel do not build walls between peoples, nor do they separate Catholics in their own societies; on the contrary, the Gospel strengthens the bonds that link man to man. Jesus Christ has come as reconciler, not just as reconciler of the few who acknowledge his message but also as reconciler of the many, wherever they may be, who populate the earth. Christ is the declared and perpetual enemy of evil, that is, the enemy of all that separates men from one another and prevents the community of men from being friends. The message of Christ enables Christians to act as reconcilers in society. They are sent into the world as brothers to all men, and their mission is to deepen the consciousness of society that men are brothers, members of the same human family.[31]

Where does this understanding of the Gospel come from? This wide understanding of brotherhood is certainly not on the surface of the Scriptures. We have to admit that in the historical situation in which the Gospel was preached it became, in fact, a principle of social division. Brotherhood was confined to Christians. There were historical reasons for this. The focus of the apostolic preaching, presenting divine salvation as the reply to the principal questionings of their times, did not bring out the meaning of the Gospel for the entire human family. (We recall here the refusal of Jesus to get involved in the social and political movements seeking to liberate his people from the occupation of a foreign power.) Neither is the wider understanding of brotherhood, authoritatively taught at Vatican II, contained in the central themes of traditional Catholic teaching. In the past Catholic theology distinguished between "supernatural brotherhood" created by the acknowledgement of Christ in faith and a certain "natural brotherhood" including all men, based on the common human nature, created by God as such, in which all shared. The men of the past had questions of their own; they experienced the threats to human life in their own way and hence, under the influence of the Spirit, they focalized the Gospel as the Good News for their own age.

What is the basis for the new teaching of the brotherhood of men? I believe that the new teaching, proposed by Vatican II, is the result of the Church's fidelity in listening to God's Word present in history. Among the significant human experiences of the present age are brotherhood and universal solidarity. These values are held by people who are admired and venerated by the present generation. The men who overcome the barriers of race, of class, of nationality and religion and who affirm their solidarity with the whole human race, the men who remain loyal to their traditions and yet embrace people of different traditions as their brothers, the men who have dedicated themselves to the service of peace and the well-being of the human family, especially in underdeveloped areas—these are the men that represent the great ideals of the present culture. These are the values celebrated in art and literature; they are celebrated either by extolling the friendship that binds man to man or by denouncing the blind and often irresistible forces that isolate a man from his fellows. All over the world Pope John was acknowledged as a sign of reconciliation: he, the man of conviction, faithful to his creed and his tradition, was willing to identify himself with the entire human race and regard all men as his brothers.

Is this experience of brotherhood and solidarity the work of the Spirit? Is it a sign of the times? Does it reveal the presence of God's Word in history and hence contain a divine message for the Church? Or is this experience of brotherhood the result of human pride? Is man here affirming his solidarity in order to look away from the sin that plagues him? Is this experience the creation of man's mind helping him to take refuge in an illusory realm where he need not face the realities of life? Is it from the Spirit or is it from man's connatural self-seeking?

Throughout this century Christians have begun to see in this experience of mankind a sign of God's redemptive presence in history. In their thought, their actions and attitudes, Christians have been willing to learn from this experience. But it was only at the Vatican Council that the whole Catholic Church, represented by her collegial hierarchy, acknowledged that the universal brotherhood of man, the great experience of the age, reveals itself, under the test of the Gospel, as a redemptive reality in which God addresses his Word to the Church.

This process which began early in this century and culminated at Vatican II was accompanied by many historical and theological studies.[32] Christian scholars became more sensitive to the universalist themes in the Scriptures, to the teaching of God's universal fatherhood and the attempts in the New Testament to spell out in universal terms the meaning of Christ's redemption. A study of the Christian tradition brought out that while the ancients held a restrictive view of the Church, their tradition contained doctrinal hints and suggestions—such as the single divine finality of human life—which, when given closer attention, eventually led to the conclusion that the Spirit-created communion between Christians in grace reaches beyond the Church to all men open to the Spirit. Ultimately, these studies could not demonstrate that this new understanding of brotherhood was in harmony with divine revelation. What counted was the experience of the Church, the dialogue and common action among Christians, a new sense of responsibility in regard to human society, and eventually the experience of the Vatican Council itself. There the assembled bishops and the pope declared their faith that universal brotherhood is a redemptive reality. God is redemptively at work wherever people are. This acknowledgement produced a re-focusing of the Gospel—or, at least, its beginning.

In addition to the experience of human solidarity I shall briefly mention the peculiar experience of Christian solidarity that the ecumenical movement has produced. This experience has also been of doctrinal importance. Here, too, the Church listened to the experience of men. Is this Christian fellowship across ecclesiastical boundaries a work of the Spirit? Or is it the work of darkness, weakening in all Christians the sense of truth and the dedication to mission? Many arguments may be drawn from Scripture and tradition to show that the brotherly association of Christians across doctrinal differences is not the work of the Spirit. We know that such arguments were invoked when the ecumenical movement began.[33] But there are also some hints in the New Testament that seem to encourage the fellowship of separated Christians. The ultimate verdict, however, that the experience of new solidarity was in harmony with the Gospel, was not the conclusion of a theological demonstration; it was, rather, the acknowledgement by the Council that the Spirit was at work in this solidarity and that God was addressing his Church through the ecumenical movement.

I have given two instances of what listening to God's Word in history has meant at Vatican II. Others could be given. The two examples reveal the doctrinal shift from a closed to an open understanding of Church. They illustrate the re-focusing of the Gospel that took place at Vatican II. By listening to God's Word proclaimed in the Church and present in the history of men, the Vatican Council announced divine revelation as the Good News to a world threatened by dividedness in personal and social life. Jesus is reconciler. God in Christ creates community among those who acknowledge him in faith and are baptized in his name; but beyond this the God who revealed himself in Christ creates community wherever people are open to one another. Wherever people are, something happens. This is the Good News. There are, indeed, the forces of destruction operating in human society; but man is not delivered over to them. Why? Because God has revealed in Jesus Christ that he is present to human life and that men, through his presence, become friends.

We now come to *the third step* in the process of re-focusing the Gospel. The process began, we remember, with the discernment of the demonic and the deepest questioning in the new spiritual-cultural environment. Then followed the attempt of the Church —by faithfully listening to God's Word in her past and her present—to present the Gospel once for all revealed as the Good News in this new environment. This attempt involved new Christian experience. It included dialogue, research, reflection. The whole Church was involved in it. Divine revelation was ultimately formulated as the salvational reply to the present predicament by an act of the ecclesiastical magisterium as the new focus of the self-identical Gospel.

The third step in this process is the re-interpretation of the entire Christian teaching in the light of the new focus. We recall that a focus of the Gospel is not simply an important doctrinal position; it is, rather, the central view, in the light of which the entire mystery of salvation is understood and which holds together, interrelates, and qualifies the entire teaching of the Church. What is required, therefore, in the process of re-focusing the Gospel is the re-reading of the Scriptures and the whole tradition of the Church in order to gain a new view of the Christian faith in its totality.

The best way of explaining this third step is to return to the doctrinal shift that took place at Vatican II. The new understanding of Church, of fellowship, of the mystery of redemption present in human life, demands a re-reading of Scripture and tradition and a re-interpretation of all the positions which, in the past, were understood as favouring a restrictive notion of Church. What does Christian teaching mean when it confines salvation to believers? When it proclaims Jesus as the unique mediator between God and men? When it calls the entry into the Church a passage from death to life? If we adopt the open understanding of Church we must re-interpret these doctrinal positions in the light of the new focus. We will have to show that saving faith is a divine gift, not confined to the Church but available to people in their openness to the Spirit. We will have to show that the unique mediation of Jesus Christ does not limit grace to the Church. We will have to show that the entry into the Church is a passage from death to life for men who had closed their ears to the Spirit and who were opened to new life through the preaching of the Gospel. Yet this passage from death to life happens not only when sinners enter the Church; it happens, in some way, whenever men who are closed in their self-centredness are summoned by God and begin to listen to him. This process of re-interpreting traditional teaching began at Vatican II.

There are other examples of a more practical nature that illustrate the need for re-interpretation. In the light of the new focus what is the meaning of baptism? Or, more difficult, what is the meaning of infant baptism? Is it still necessary? What about the mission of the Church? What is the mission Christ assigned to the Church if God is redemptively involved in human life everywhere? What is the mission of the Church if the saving action of God is already at work among people offering them new life —as persons and as community? Related to this is the question of how to distinguish between Church and world. The affirmation of the open Church does not obliterate the distinction between Church and world! But the new focus does demand that the difference between Church and world be re-interpreted in the light of the new insight.

Catholic theologians have dealt with many of these questions. They do not always agree in their interpretations. Many questions remain open. It is my conviction that the re-focusing that has taken place at Vatican II leads to a re-interpretation even of the notion of God, in particular of the divine transcendence. We note here—and we shall have occasion to come back to it further on—that some of the doctrinal uncertainty in the Catholic Church at this time is precisely due to the fact that a re-focusing of the Gospel has taken place, but that the subsequent re-interpretation of Christian teaching has not been fully achieved. The process of re-interpretation is a gradual one.

Is there a further step in the re-focusing of the Gospel? Is there a fourth step in which traditional teaching is translated into the language and the concepts proper to the new spiritual-cultural environment? We recall that the "accommodated preaching of the divine Word"—which Vatican II called "the law of all evangelization"—asks for the proclamation of the Gospel in terms taken from contemporary culture. My point in this connection is that what has taken place in steps one, two, and three is not only a new way of focusing the Gospel and understanding it as the divine answer to men's deepest questionings; it is, at the same time, the translation of the Gospel into language and concepts of the present. Step one, we recall, consists in discerning the crucial questions of people. Already in this step the Church deals with issues that trouble her contemporaries and hence, inevitably, thinks in contemporary terms. In step two the Church listens to the experience of the world and tries to discern in it the presence of God's Word. The Church tries to find the divine reply to the present predicament as the focus that will make her message the Good News for the present. Inevitably, this will be expressed in a language and in concepts taken from contemporary cultural experience. The third step, the re-interpretation of Christian teaching in the light of the new focus, enables the Church to speak of the whole of Christian teaching in new terms proper to the culture in which she lives and in which she preaches. We conclude, therefore, that with these three steps the Gospel has been translated into a new cultural language.

We note that this process of re-interpretation is the very contrary of a cultural assimilation of the Gospel. This translation or —to use the word of Vatican II—this "accommodation" is not the work of man's intelligence at home in the meaning of language and the mutation of concepts. The translation is brought about by the Church's effort to be faithful to the divine Word. It is a response in faith. It begins by discovering the dimensions of evil in the present age. Even when, in the second step, the present culture is seen in its positive elements the discernment takes place in the light of the apostolic witness. The apostolic witness remains normative in the entire process. The divine Word in history is acknowledged precisely because it is identical with the Word of God present in the apostolic witness. The identity is discerned, we said, not simply through intellectual analysis; the discernment takes place in a creative process, the Spirit-created experience of the Church in which the Word addressed to her in the present is recognized as the Word spoken once for all in Jesus Christ. This is what is meant by "infallibility".

If I understand Leslie Dewart's theory of doctrinal development[34] correctly I find that I come to the same conclusions, even if our methods of investigation have been quite different. Dewart insists that if the Church wants to be faithful to the Gospel, once-for-all received, in a new cultural age, she must "re-conceptualize" it—or, in our terminology, re-focus and re-interpret it; if she simply repeats what she said in the past she will, in fact, no longer announce the same Gospel. This re-conceptualization is not achieved as the intellectual task of translating the creeds and doctrinal formulas into a new cultural and philosophical language. What must happen is something more original and creative. Dewart rightly insists that re-conceptualization is the faithful response of the Church to the divine Word addressed to her in the present. Divine revelation, though definitive and exhaustive in Jesus Christ—and from this point of view closed—continues in the Church: God continues to speak his self-identical Word in the Church. This on-going self-communication of God in his Word evokes the faith of the Church and thus constitutes her in her being as the community of the faithful. For Dewart, therefore, the re-conceptualization of divine revelation is a process by which the Church, faithful to the apostolic witness and at home in a new cultural environment, responds in faith to the divine Word spoken in her and to her. The re-conceptualization of revelation is the new self-consciousness of the Church.

This concludes our examination of the tension between past and present, implicit in the Gospel. It has been my point that the

Catholic Church, because of her acknowledgment of divine tradition, has retained the tension between past and present. She is not irretrievably tied to the past, neither to the 1st century nor to the consensus of the first five centuries, nor to the doctrinal crystallization of the 16th century. She is faithful to the past, but not tied to it. She acknowledges the Word of God spoken to her in the present and hence is able to re-interpret the self-identical Gospel as the Good News for the contemporary world: this Spirit-created capacity of the Church to detect God's present self-communication to her by its identity with the Word once delivered, a capacity which involves her Christian experience and eventually a doctrinal consensus through pope and bishops, may be called her "infallibility". Thanks to this "infallibility", the Catholic Church remains open to the future.

We have here a second meaning of Open Church. Because the events of salvation took place almost 2000 years ago, the Christian Church often appears as oriented toward the past. She seems to reflect on the past; she seems to think that what is really important happened a long time ago and hence not to expect good things to happen tomorrow. Must the Church always be oriented toward the past? Is not the Gospel full of promises of about tomorrow and the day after tomorrow? The theological reflections in these pages have tried to show that the past events, once for all recorded in the Scriptures, enable the Church to discern the Word of God addressed to her in the present and hence to open herself to the future into which she moves. Living out the tension between past and present, the Church opens herself to the future and finds a way of speaking about God and his Son Jesus Christ that makes sense to the secular culture of tomorrow.

We close this chapter with a concluding paragraph. We have

said that the Catholic Church, especially in her claim to uniqueness, is credible if she is meaningful in terms of the New Testament, if she explains the past, and if she illuminates present experience. We have seen that the Catholic claim to uniqueness is meaningful in terms of the tensions, given in the New Testament, between the local and the universal and between the past and the present. We have seen that the fidelity to these tensions is assured by the social dynamics of the collegial structure (pope and bishops) and the acknowledgement of a creative element in handing on the Gospel (divine tradition). This explains why the Catholic Church has defended these two elements of her life so vehemently in the past. We have seen, moreover, that the claim to uniqueness illumines present experience: for the Catholic Church alone is, at this time, capable of a doctrinal consensus received as normative by her members and, because of this and because of her acknowledgment of God's Word in the present (infallibility), capable of re-interpreting the Gospel as the Good News for men in our day. Doctrinal consensus and re-interpretation of the Gospel happened at the Vatican Council. Her claim to uniqueness enables the Catholic Church to make a special contribution to the ecumenical movement.

5.

The Church of Tomorrow

CHARLES Davis' first argument against the Catholic Church, we recall, was a demonstration that her self-understanding lacked all credibility. We have dealt with this argument in the preceding chapters. Charles Davis' second argument is more interesting.[1] He thinks that in the future all the Churches will disappear. He believes that the changes taking place in the world and in human self-understanding are such that the institutional Churches will no longer be adequate instruments for the promotion of Christian life. In his *A Question of Conscience* Davis emphasizes that his protest against the Catholic Church and the other Churches is not made in the name of a Christian individualism. It does not occur to him to suggest that a man can be a Christian alone. He acknowledges that to be Christian means to belong to a community. The Gospel creates community. Charles Davis explains that he is not opposed to institutions as such, not even against religious institutions. He thinks that social institutions are necessary to people: they express community of life and they promote it. The common meaning people experience in their lives finds expression in social institutions which communicate and intensify this meaning. Precisely because Charles Davis acknowledges the social reality of life he thinks that the institutional Churches, Catholic and otherwise, will disintegrate in the future. Christian life, Christian social life will be expressed and communicated through social institutions of another type.

How does Charles Davis substantiate his position? First he shows that in our times men are acquiring a new self-understanding. In the past we tended to understand ourselves according to a static and rationally definable human nature, and we regarded life as the actualization of capacities and principles implicit in this nature. Today, because of a cultural and social evolution, we tend to understand ourselves in terms of personal being historically achieved, and therefore look upon life as the realization of human responses to reality. Human life is open-ended. Man is not defined by his nature. In his life man is summoned to assume greater responsibility for himself and freed to create his own future.

Corresponding to man's self-understanding is his ideal of society. Charles Davis shows that these two ways of understanding man give rise to two distinct types of social organization. Men who understand themselves in terms of a rationally definable nature project their social body as a static hierarchical society. This has been the ideal of society until modern times. When men begin to understand themselves as personal beings open to the future and responsible for who they will be, the ideal of social organization undergoes a radical change. The older hierarchical types of society are no longer able to express the community of life which people enjoy and seek to promote. According to Charles Davis, the new type of social organization has three typical characteristics. *First,* these social organizations are created by people for the sake of handling particular aspects of their

THE CHURCH OF TOMORROW

social life. Institutions do not precede life. People engaged in a common life and meaning create for themselves a variety of institutions to promote particular activities and services that they judge necessary. *Secondly,* these organizations will never embrace the whole of a man's life. Their concern will be strictly limited to one aspect of life, that aspect for the sake of which they were created. For this reason people never totally belong to any institution. They will participate in various institutions depending on their areas of responsibility and their interests, but they will always remain sufficiently independent of these institutions and thus remain free to determine their own future. The new self-understanding of man demands that his involvement in the institutional life will not prevent him from choosing his personal future. *Thirdly,* the social organizations corresponding to the new self-understanding of man remain radically changeable. They are always provisional. They are created for a particular purpose and when this purpose disappears or is modified then the institutions designed to serve it must also go or be radically changed.

Charles Davis comes to the following conclusion. All the Christian Churches have an institutional structure that corresponds to the old self-understanding of man. Whatever the system, whether Catholic, Anglican, or Protestant, the ecclesiastical institutions are static and hierarchical. As Christians assume the new self-understanding it is inevitable that the old institutions will disintegrate. The Christians of the future will not be able to·live out the Gospel in them. The future of the Church depends on the creation of new social organizations, corresponding to the new self-understanding of man. The Gospel creates community. The Christian life demands cooperation, interrelation, mutuality . . . Institutions are necessary for the Church of the future; but they will be created by Christians as they need them, they will not embrace the whole of a man's life but leave him free to choose his own personal future, and they will be provisional and temporary.

Charles Davis thinks, therefore, that the Churches will fall apart. He thinks that there is enough historical evidence to say that large institutions never have the inner resources to make radical changes. Either they disintegrate and die, or else they are changed by revolutions. It is inconceivable, he thinks, that the Churches will be able to adapt to the changing needs of the Christian community. They will defend their power structures, and by thus preferring themselves to their people they will be swept away by the flow of history—either by falling apart as societies altogether or by saving themselves as small sectarian bodies outside the stream of life.

THE RESTLESS CHURCH

WHAT are we to think of this analysis of the present state of affairs? I agree with Charles Davis' description of man's new self-understanding and I am also convinced that this new self-understanding will have a profound effect on the organizational patterns of ecclesiastical life. Yet the conclusion that the Churches will inevitably crumble to pieces I find—for reasons to be explained later—extreme and unconvincing.

The changing self-understanding of man and the inevitable effect of this on his institutional life is a subject that is not peculiar to Charles Davis. He gives witness to preoccupations that are shared by all thinkers today including Catholic theologians. A few months prior to the publication of *A Question of Conscience* I wrote an article for *The Ecumenist*[2] in which I examined the cause for the restlessness in the Church and came to the conclusion that the new self-understanding of Christians demands new institutional patterns in the Church. My final conclusion differed from that of Charles Davis because I thought that the Vatican Council had acknowledged the need for new patterns and had made participation the key-concept for the reform of the Church's institutional life. I admitted that this ideal existed mainly on paper. Since the short article resembled the thinking of Charles Davis—except for his final conclusion—I want to ask the reader's indulgence and cite the principal sections of the article in the following pages.

It seems to me that the restlessness in the Catholic Church is due to a new self-understanding that is emerging among Christians. Our theological anthropology has undergone a significant development. Through the biblical movement, through dialogue with contemporary philosophy, and through man's participation in the new conditions of the modern world, a theological understanding of man has evolved in Catholic literature that was able to express itself in the documents of Vatican Council II, especially in the *Constitution on Divine Revelation* and the *Pastoral Constitution on the Church in the Modern World*. What is happening at the moment is that the anthropology proposed in the conciliar documents as a doctrine, is being assimilated by Christians as personal knowledge and hence is beginning to determine their own self-understanding.

How can this new anthropology be described? I will attempt a brief sketch of it, a schematic description to convey the idea to the reader who, from his reading and his own personal experience, knows what I am talking about.

Man Is a Listener. As God reveals himself as the One who

181

addresses man in his Word, so he reveals man to himself as one who is meant to listen. Man is open to what others communicate to him, and he will never cease to be a learner. Man listens to other people; and through these others he is able to listen to the world, to history, and even to God. According to biblical teaching, God communicates himself to men through human speech and human gestures: Word and sacrament as mediated by men are the matrix of man's relationship to God.

Saying that man is a listener is different from saying that he is a knower. When man is called a knower then his vis-à-vis is truth, possibly abstract, impersonal truth. When man is called a listener then his vis-à-vis is always a person. We listen to someone. Listening relates us to someone who has something to say to us.

As a listener man realizes that he is only beginning to understand what life is all about. He is always ready to learn more. He enters every situation expecting to learn something new. He wants to be sensitive to the summons that comes to him from his relationship to people and from his situation in the world. He is even ready to listen to the unconditional call that comes to him as God's Word. For this reason man is unwilling to tie himself to any position that will prevent him from being a listener. Deep religious convictions are acceptable to him only if they allow him to remain open to other people. Today we distinguish clearly between faith and fanaticism. Religious convictions are regarded as fanatical when they prevent a man from being open to others, block his ears, and always make him misunderstand what others are saying.

The Personal Structure of Man is Dialogical. Man comes to be a person through dialogue with others. Man is a listener summoned to respond, and his responses constitute him in his personal being. Man is not a finished substance whose life simply actualizes what is potentially contained in him. The principle *agere sequitur esse* applies to things, to animals, and to machines: it does not always apply to man. Man is an open-ended being. He is involved in an unending dialogue which makes him to be who he is. Man is forever led into new situations, he listens to a summons that does not come from himself and by responding to it he determines his existence as a person.

In Jesus Christ, God has revealed his purpose to enter into a dialogue of salvation with every single human being.[3] Wherever a man is, in the Church or outside of it, he lives in a situation that is salvational. He is addressed by a call or challenge, the absolute character of which betrays its transcendent origin. God is Word, eternal Word: God is always One who addresses himself to men. For this reason we affirm that human life is supernatural. Human life is not simply the living out of man's nature; it is the realization of man's dialogue of salvation with God.

The man who is open to dialogue is nourished by God. God redeems man, sanctifies or humanizes him, through dialogue. God acts in the world through the conversation and association of men.

Man Grows Through a Process of Conversions. A man does not want to remain as he is. He always wants to change and grow. He seeks to become more truly himself. For this reason he desires to come to self-knowledge. He wants to know who he is. He wishes to face all that is in him, even the destructive, even the sinful, with utmost sincerity. He realizes that he cannot change himself by his own will power. He might be able to force himself to do this or that, but he cannot give himself the freedom to forget himself and be concerned about others. The important changes in a man's life will have to happen to him,

183

happen as the result of his listening and his involvement with others.

Man is not simply an intelligent agent who comes to knowledge by learning objective truth. Coming to a knowledge that counts always implies a re-orientation of a man's life. Insight comes through a process of conversion. This is true for Christians and non-Christians alike. Wherever people are, they are summoned to growth, to leave their childish past behind, and to assume greater responsibility for themselves and for their environment. This repeated re-orientation of a person's life toward reality demands a great price. Conversion always hurts. It demands the abandoning of many things that are dear to us. At the same time, conversion is always experienced as a reply to a call that comes from beyond ourselves. The important changes in human life are never experienced as being self-initiated. They are grace.

Man Is in Need of the Community to Become Himself. The dialogical personal structure of man indicates that his inner reality has been received by him from others. His speech, his feelings, his knowledge would never have developed without mother, father and other people who came close to him. What is true of early childhood is true of later life. Man needs the community to fulfill his destiny. Without the help of his brothers, and ultimately of the whole human family, man cannot exercise his divine vocation of reconciling and humanizing life on earth. Man must therefore be politically involved.

This personalistic understanding of man is quite different from the individualism that we find in some authors of the past. Man is not an individual who grows by focusing on himself. Man does not achieve well-being by straining narcissistically after self-fulfillment. Man is a person, and hence he becomes more truly himself through communion with others. The center of man is outside of himself.

This community aspect of the human person also discloses a new understanding of the human body. Man is inserted into the community through his body. His body is the instrument of communication with people. The body may not simply be regarded as a physical substructure of the spiritual soul; it must be understood as a more truly human reality. It is the locus of man's presence to other people and to the world. The new self-understanding of man leads him to a new way of experiencing his bodiliness, its meaning and role in his life.

Man's Life Is Constantly Threatened. Man is exposed to forces that could undo him. These forces could prevent a man from being a listener; they could keep him from entering deeply into dialogue and from growing up through repeated conversions; they could prevent him from entering into communion with others. Man is threatened by the outer and inner situation of his life to become unfaithful to the divine call of becoming truly human.

The task of the Gospel is to reveal to man the forces that threaten his human existence and to offer him access to a communion, a divine communion, that enables him to be faithful to his call and destiny. The Gospel does not offer a ready-made blueprint of the good life. It does not solve all of man's problems in advance. It leaves many moral and intellectual questions unsolved. What the Gospel lays bare are the forces that could destroy man and what it offers as a remedy are the sources that enable a man to become a listener, to enter into dialogue, to be ready for conversion and growth, and to participate in the life of the community. This is the present salvation brought by Christ.

185

This is a brief sketch of the theological anthropology that has emerged in the Catholic Church. I have mentioned that this happened through the biblical movement, through dialogue with contemporary thought and through experience in the new conditions of the modern world. According to Vatican II, "The human race has passed from a rather static conception of reality to a more dynamic, evolutionary one."[4] What is happening at the moment is that this teaching is being assimilated as self-knowledge. People are beginning to experience themselves in this way. Their new self-understanding determines their conscious actions and their reflective knowledge of reality.

In the past the understanding of man taught by the Church—and hence the self-understanding of her members—was somewhat different. It is not my intention here to describe the theological anthropology that characterized the recent past. Our understanding of man was certainly more static. Divine revelation was not so much regarded as God's self-disclosure with the concomitant disclosure of man to himself; it was, rather, considered as the divine teaching on faith and morals. These mapped out the course of human life.

Since institutions are made to promote man's life in society, they inevitably reflect the understanding of man that is current at the time they are created. The institutions in the Church—seminaries, monasteries, convents, ecclesiastical government, and law courts—embody and promote the ideal of man as it was conceived at the time when they received their definitive shape. What is happening today is that with a new self-understanding many Christians find that these institutions of the Church operate on an anthropology that is no longer ours. In the past a seminarian leaving the seminary might have said to his rector, "Your ideal is too high for me. I don't think I can live up to it". Today the seminarian who leaves the seminary often says, "I don't want to be the kind of person this institution makes me into. I want to be someone different". This does not mean that the men responsible for the institution were lacking in generosity and kindness. With his remark the seminarian does not wish to accuse anyone. What he wants to say is that the anthropology implicit in the institutional pattern does not correspond to his own Christian self-understanding.

This evolution gives rise to a crisis. Even among priests and nuns who made their vows many years ago we find some whose self-understanding has changed so much that they no longer want to be the kind of person they wanted to be a few years ago. Some of them are convinced that they cannot be faithful to their vocation as human beings in the institutions they entered with so much love at one time. We have in the Church the unusual phenomenon that many priests and nuns are leaving their chosen way of life, not with a feeling that they are thereby unfaithful to a high calling but, rather, with the conviction that their choice is an act of fidelity to the human growth which the Spirit is producing in them. It is time for the institutions to reflect on their responsibility for this sort of crisis.

Vatican II as an institution was a manifestation of the new self-understanding of man! At least it became that through the dynamics of the conciliar process. Those who participated became listeners, were drawn into dialogue, became ready to change their ways, and had a new experience of fellowship and joint responsibility. Vatican II attempted to modify ecclesiastical institutions by making them correspond to the new anthropology. The liturgy (in the vernacular) was to make men into listeners and brothers. Participation was the key concept that inspired all the changes in institutions, whether these had to do with worship, ministry, religious life, or ecclesiastical government. Institutions in the Church must allow Christians to participate; and it is through the very process of participation that men are renewed, made sensitive to the Spirit, and open to one another. This ideal of participation in ecclesiastical institutions exists, so far, mainly on paper.

It is not easy to translate the ideals of Vatican Council II into reality. It seems to me that the new forms which ecclesiastical institutions must take will have to be developed by the people who have acquired the new self-understanding. New institutional forms cannot be invented by canon lawyers uninvolved in the kind of life these institutions intend to promote. On the contrary, it is the people living the life that must give shape to the institutional forms that serve them, and it is in this process of finding the best institutional forms that men are drawn into participation and begin to experience themselves in a new way. The future will demand many experiments in social living. A new code of canon law and slightly modified structures which then become as rigid as the old ones, will not relieve the restlessness in the Church. As Church, as God's pilgrim people, we will have to develop a greater sense of the provisional.

*　　*　　*

Vatican II acknowledges the effect of man's new self-understanding on his social organizations by making participation the key-concept for all institutional changes. This thesis could be developed at length. The teaching of the Council on collegiality, at first strongly resisted by the conservative minority, introduced a dialogue structure into the exercise of authority on the highest ecclesiastical level. Collegiality means—we saw this in an earlier chapter—that the bishops are co-responsible with the pope for the teaching and policy-making of the Catholic Church. Prior to Vatican II "the powers" of the hierarchy in the Catholic system were divided into the power to celebrate the sacraments (*potestas ordinis*) and the power to legislate (*potestas iurisdictionis*). Vatican II has changed this. The collegial authority of the bishops is neither *potestas ordinis* nor *potestatas iurisdictiones*. It is the acknowledgement of team responsibility that transcends the traditional understanding of power in the Catholic Church.[5] This collegiality or team responsibility is operative not only when the bishops collaborate with the pope in matters relating to the whole Church; it operates also when the bishops of a province, nation, or continent collaborate to solve the common pastoral problems. The dialogue structure in the exercise of authority is acknowledged for every level of the ecclesiastical institution. The Vatican Council retains the bishop as the only legislator in his diocese; at the same time by introducing the ideal of team responsibility, it modifies the system sufficiently to allow for the participation of clergy and laity in teaching and policy-making.[6] On the basis of the sacramental unity between the bishop and his priests (*unum presbyterium*[7]), priests are called to participate in the teaching and governing that belongs to the bishop in his diocese. On the basis of the unity of the Church and the presence of the Spirit to her the Christian people are called to participation: they are to be consulted, they are to express themselves freely, they may be in dialogue with the bishop and his clergy through synods and other institutions. Even in the reform of religious orders Vatican II acknowledges the participation of all the members in decisions that will affect their lives.[8]

The participation advocated by Vatican II enters the life of the Church very slowly. Superiors stake out the region in which they will permit participation but the decisions which they regard as important they still tend to make alone. The Vatican Council itself was perhaps the only ecclesiastical instance where participation was a concrete political reality including diversity of opinions and the inevitable tensions. But the transition from a monarchical to a collegial exercise of authority in ordinary ecclesiastical life seems to meet enormous obstacles. Will it ever happen?

While the Vatican Council advocated participation as the ideal, it reserved the decision-making ultimately to a few people living in a single city. This state of affairs has no doctrinal basis. The history of the Church records a variety of ways in which authority was exercised and in which decisions regarding policy were reached. The papal-episcopal (collegial) structure can function in many ways. It is capable of adaptation to the needs of the Christian people. There is in the Catholic Church not only development of doctrine; there is also development of structure. And as there are moments in the history of the Church—as she enters a new spiritual-cultural environment—when doctrinal development is non-homogeneous, the structural development in the Church need not always be thought of as homogeneous. The papal-episcopal structure, given by Christ in the Spirit to his people, is capable of adaptations which permit the kind of participation that seems proper and responsible to men of the present culture—and of any culture. Affirming, in this connection, the universality of the Catholic Church and the presence of the Spirit to her means precisely this: the collegial structure, Christ-given as we believe, is a living reality that may be made to respond to the needs of the Christian people and their ideals of social organization of any age whatever.

This leads us to the question of Charles Davis. Can a powerful establishment ever change? Are the governmental systems in the Catholic Church and the other Churches ready to adapt to the changing self-understanding of man? Can existing institutions become flexible and respond to the new needs of the people whom they serve? Charles Davis thinks not. The Churches, he believes, are committed to static structures. Institutions with position and power never abandon their privileged situation voluntarily. As history moves on they will either fall apart or be transformed by revolutions.

It seems to me that Charles Davis comes to his conclusion too quickly. Neither sociologically nor theologically has the ecclesiastical problem of structural development been carefully studied. How can anyone arrive at a speedy conclusion, especially at such a radical one?

First of all we know very little of the sociology of structural change in the Churches. Charles Davis applies an analogy drawn from the Marxist analysis of social transformation: the inner dynamics of society creates a tension between the people and their rulers until eventually, through an historical process, a point is reached when revolution is the only manner of resolving the conflict and of assuring the life of the people. The passage from static to dynamic structures can come about only through radical discontinuity. Even if—for the sake of argument—one accepted this theory for the evolution of political societies, there seems to be no evidence at all that it is applicable, without qualifications, to religious institutions. Religious institutions in the modern world are free-will organizations. Sociologically, they are held together by the good will of the people who belong to them. It is true that, theologically speaking, this good will is God's gracious gift to men, and therefore the Church as community is created, not by men but by God's living Word evoking the faith of the community. Yet sociologically speaking the Church remains a free-will organization, even if the free will that brings people together is the divine self-communication to men. Since, in this sense, the ecclesiastical society is based on the free will of her members, the laws that apply to societies created by national and economic necessity cannot simply be carried over to the Church. Because, sociologically speaking, people are free to leave the Churches, at least in modern society, the relations between ruler and ruled in the Church are quite different from their counterparts in political societies. Conflicts and tensions in the Church may be worked out in ways that are not open in a political society to which people must belong by necessity.

Secondly, I suggest, we know very little about structural change in the Church from a theological point of view. We have no theology of change! As we saw in chapter two, the Western Christian tradition has interpreted God's gift of himself in Christ mainly in terms of what happens to persons, and hardly in terms of what happens to society. We have analyzed sin, grace, conversion, sanctification, in personal terms; but we have not reflected much on what the need of redemption means for man's social life. How does God's presence to human life change the community? What does grace, conversion, sanctification mean when applied to man's social existence? These are questions which we cannot yet answer. It seems to me, therefore, that Charles Davis' extreme conclusion is not the result of a careful sociological or theological inquiry.

I wish to add at this point that we are greatly in need of a theology of change. One of the reasons why the present changes in Catholic life are so frightening to many people is that there is no theology initiating them into the meaning of change and providing principles whereby changes may be evaluated.

A New Sociological Model for the Church

How will the new self-understanding of man affect the social organizations of the Church? Are we able to foresee in which direction the Church will move? Catholics have begun to speculate on this question.

Among some Catholics deeply concerned with reform and renewal we find the desire to introduce into the ecclesiastical institution the democratic processes developed in modern society.[9] They foresee a vast conciliar system, parish councils, diocesan councils, national councils, and more universal councils, in which the representatives of various groups in the Church can make their voices heard and contribute to the making of public policy. The final decisions will be made by the bishops and the pope through processes that involve the lower clergy and the people and at the same time preserve the special role and power of the episcopal college. Foreseen is a legislation in the Church protecting the rights of individual Christians and their societies against undue interference by higher superiors. The principle of subsidiarity will be guaranteed by law. For the better functioning of the Church there will be law courts to which Christians may appeal if they have not been justly treated according to the common law of the Church.

Canon law societies and individual canon lawyers have already worked out various projects for the institutional Church of the future, and outlined the nature and the form which constitutional law should take in this Church.[10] In all of these, modern concepts of government play a great role. These projects may vary as to the amount of independent action they ascribe to the hierarchy in the process of decision-making. Some canonists think

it desirable, and possible, that the Catholic Church adopt a constitution, parallel to civil society, which limits the power of the
ecclesiastical government according to common law. In other
words, there are Catholic theologians and canonists who believe
that it is in harmony with the Catholic understanding of the
Church's divine foundation and the apostolic succession of
the episcopal college (pope and bishops) to advocate the creation
of a constitutional papacy and constitutional episcopacy.

This interpretation of the structural development taking place
in the Church is clearly based on the historical experience of
Western society. From a highly diversified and many-leveled
feudalism, Western society passed into the age of the absolute
monarchy. Then, under the pressure of national life, the king
created councils or parliaments and permitted the people or their
representatives to have an increasingly greater share in the
making of his own decisions. Eventually the affirmation of the
citizens' power transformed deliberative councils into legislative
assemblies. This was the common road of Western society to
constitutional monarchies and the republican state.

There are undoubtedly signs that a similar kind of development has taken place in the Churches. The Catholic Church has
resisted this development and until recently her methods of government reflected political institutions which are no longer with
us. In particular, there is in the Catholic Church no separation
between the legislative and judicial offices. The desire for a
constitutional Church, then, is born of the conviction that the
experience of Western society is being relived in the Catholic
Church, and that what is happening at this time is the structural
perfection of the Church as a spiritual republic.

What are we to think of this interpretation of the structural
development in the Church? There are many Catholics, among

them bishops, who regard the perfections of the Church as a replica of a well-functioning modern state as the ideal for which to strive.

I have great difficulties with this view, both as an ideal and as a description of what is happening at this time in the Catholic Church. I have great difficulties in thinking of the Church as a spiritual replica of political society. In other words, I wonder whether in the present age the political society is the "sociological model" for describing the Church's institutional reality. In the first place, I do not think it would be desirable to have a Church that is a spiritual republic in which all members are involved in policy-making and the perfection of the ecclesiastical organization. In such a situation every Christian would be involved in ecclesiastical life—he would spend much of his time and ingenuity in making decisions regarding the organizational life of the Church. Every Christian would become a kind of ecclesiastical person. It seems to me, however, that the task of the Christian is to live in the world and to give his time and intelligence to the transformation of the civil society to which he belongs—and of the whole of mankind. The Gospel and its celebration in the Church should not withdraw the Christian from his involvement in secular society but should free him to serve his community in new ways and with greater dedication. If the Church were the ideal spiritual republic which we have described, she would face the civil society as a kind of spiritual duplication of itself, she would face civil society as another society. This has been true in the history of the Church for a long time. But one may wonder whether a structure which makes the Church face the secular society as a parallel sort of society, even though spiritual, does not create many undesirable effects today. A Christian then belongs to two societies and his loyalties will be strained, if not divided. In such a situation the Church would take him out of his secular life into her own, rather than intensify his participation in the society to which he belongs. In such a situation the institutional Church may become a drain in the lives of men: it would demand intellectual, personal, and financial resources for the building up of the spiritual replica of society, which would become an enormously complex ecclesiastical bureaucracy.

I wish to propose another sociological model for the institutional life of the Church which corresponds more faithfully to the contemporary understanding of the Christian involvement in secular life and describes more realistically, I think, what is beginning to happen in the Catholic Church. This new sociological model is the movement.

There are many kinds of movements in society and it may not be easy to find a single set of characteristics which define what a movement is. Some movements are inner-oriented. Some movements, that is to say, have the purpose of transforming the people who belong to it. The life and action of such a movement are designed to affect those who participate in it. Alcoholics Anonymous, for instance, is such a movement. Its purpose is to heal people with an alcoholic problem. Other movements are outer-oriented. Their purpose is to transform the society in which they exist. The life and action of such movements are designed to affect the whole of society. An outer-oriented movement also affects its own members but this effect is subordinated to the wider aim of influencing the entire community of men. An outer-oriented movement cannot be defined with reference to itself. Its essence cannot be described simply by indicating the interrelationship of the people who belong to it. In order to define an outer-oriented movement one must speak of the whole of society and indicate the role which the movement is designed to play in it. In other words, an outer-oriented movement is defined by its mission. The movement may educate its members, create fellowship among them, organize them in various groups and associations, but this inner activity is subordinated to the purpose of the movement which is to have a transforming effect on the whole of society. A political party, to give one example, is such an outer-oriented movement. It can be defined only with reference to the whole of society. While it has an effect on the people who are variously associated with it, its main purpose is to transform the political life of the entire country.

It seems to me that the outer-oriented movement may be a useful sociological model for the Church of tomorrow. The Open Church, as understood by Vatican II, is not a segregated people. The Spirit-created fellowship in the Church extends to other people, to the baptized generally and to people wherever they are, who are led by the Spirit. The Open Church is a reconciler in society. The Open Church wants to involve the whole of society in conversation. The Open Church is in solidarity with the human community in which it lives; it wants to bear the burden with others; it wants to help solve the problems from which people suffer; it realizes that the redemptive mystery—"the kingdom"—which it serves is a gracious reality that pervades human life and that gains a deeper hold on people everywhere as they enter more deeply into conversation, cooperation, and unity. The Open Church, therefore, cannot be defined in terms intrinsic to itself. It must be defined in terms of the whole human race and of its role in it. The fellowship the Open Church creates among her members and the holiness into which she initiates them are subordinated to the transforming effect of the Christian community on the society in which it lives.

197

An outer-oriented movement is defined in reference to the society in which it exists. A movement may want to grow and become stronger, it may want to attract more members; but it does not envisage including all people and identifying itself with society. A movement wants to be a lively, intelligent, and active group within society, having a profound effect on the well-being and growth of the entire social life of people.

The sociological model of the outer-oriented movement seems particularly apt to describe the Open Church of Vatican II and the changing concept of the Church's mission. However varied the concept of mission may still be in Catholic theology, all theologians agree that the Church's mission cannot be defined in terms of the salvation the Church offers to men who, without her, would be eternally lost.[11] Vatican II has affirmed God's redemptive involvement in human life everywhere. The mission of the Church is to unify and reconcile the human family in the power of the Gospel. There is disagreement among Catholic theologians as to what precisely this means. It is possible to understand this mission as the witness of the Church in dialogue and cooperation by which she serves the redemptive mystery present in others, and in doing so mediates to them as well as to herself the freedom to enter more deeply into man's divine destiny. Since the Gospel reveals the sickness of society and makes available the sources of well-being, the Church's mission is a movement of humanization. The Gospel is a critique of human life. The mission of the Church, therefore, is to serve mankind with this Gospel and to help the redemptive presence of God among people to triumph in terms of unity, reconciliation, social justice, and peace. The Church wants to be a strong movement. She hopes to attract people to join her in faith and dedicate themselves with her to serve the kingdom mysteriously present in human society. But the Church after Vatican II also acknowledges the pluralistic world in which we live as good and has no intention of becoming co-extensive with the society in which she lives. She wants to be an outer-oriented movement in society.

Another characteristic of a movement is that there are many ways of belonging to it. People involve themselves in a movement in different ways, depending on their gifts and interests, on their situation in life, and on their ideals at the particular time. They may become active and assume responsibility in it; they may attend all the meetings and read the literature; but they may also choose to have a rather limited contact with the institutional centre of the movement and simply follow its thinking, reflect on its wisdom, and endorse its ideals in their association with other people. A movement does not have a clearly defined membership. People choose their own way of being involved in it. Some people who have little organizational contact with the movement may, nonetheless, be deeply touched by its ideals which have a profound effect on society and thus, in their own way, promote the purpose for which the movement exists.

In this a movement differs from a society. A society has a clearly defined membership. You always know whether you belong to it or not. You are a member of a society, not by a particular function or by the work you do, but simply by being assigned a particular place in the society, by having your name written into a book. If you are a member of a society you remain a member, even if your involvement becomes minimal—as long as you do not take your name off the list. A society is sociologically visible in all of its members. A society has clearly defined boundaries. A movement does not have visible boundary lines.

It seems to me that the Catholic Church, in these days of evolution, is becoming a social movement. People involve themselves in the life of the Church in different ways and in different degrees. At a time when the teaching of the Church encouraged Catholics to believe that divine grace was operative principally within the Church, an attitude was generated that produced clearly defined boundary lines around the Church. Either you belonged to it or you did not. You always knew whether you were in it or out of it. But today when we teach that the redemptive mystery is present to human life and communicated wherever people are open to one another, the boundaries of the Church are not so clearly visible. The Church is still a visible community, the community of those who announce and celebrate this mystery, but since she extends her fellowship to others and wants to identify herself in solidarity with the whole community, she no longer generates the attitude that draws up strict boundary lines. People have begun to involve themselves in ecclesiastical life in a variety of ways. It is not always as easy as it was in the past to know whether a man is a member of the Church.

There may be good reasons for regretting this development. It seems to me, however, that this shift from society to movement is already taking place in the Catholic Church. This is the open Church in the making.

In this connection we must examine a wide-spread phenomenon in the Catholic Church that has been called "the third man". The term goes back to François Roustang's article "Le troisième homme", published in the French Jesuit review *Christus*,[12] which has been widely acknowledged in the Catholic Church. The article describes the creation of a new kind of man in the Church. There are in the Church progressive Catholics who wish to renew Catholic life according to Vatican II, then there are conservative Catholics who prefer the preconciliar Church, and finally there is "the third man". Who is this third man? The third man believes that God has acted in Jesus Christ on behalf of all men and that this divine salvation is available in the Spirit in the celebration of the Catholic Church. The third man is a Catholic. He regards the Church as his spiritual home. He is deeply attached to the Catholic tradition. At the same time, he takes the institutional Church with a grain of salt. He loves Catholic teaching when it makes sense to him, when it gives him access to new life and enables him to respond to the demands the world makes on him; but if the teaching does not make sense to him, he does not bother with it. He does not wish to argue with other Catholics about it. It would not occur to him to argue with the bishops or the pope. If these teachings make sense to other Catholics, the third man thinks they should accept them whole-heartedly. Similarly, the third man loves the sacramental life of the Church. He participates in the sacraments when they make sense to him, when they deepen his awareness of God's presence and strengthen him in his involvement with other people. But when they do not make sense to him, when they become barriers to worship and to community, then he does not bother with them. Again, he does not feel like arguing about it. He makes his own choice; he does not feel guilty about it. He wants to leave other people free to make up their own minds. The third man, moreover, acknowledges the law of the Church. He is no rebel. He believes in law and order. At the same time, he realizes that human life is complex and that there are situations in which ecclesiastical law does not promote the spiritual well-being of persons. In those cases he feels free to act apart from canon law and, if necessary, move to the margin of the ecclesiastical institution.

What are we to think of the third man? The question is an important one since the ecclesiastical phenomenon is very widely spread in the North American Church. The third man, as first analysed by François Roustang and then acknowledged in Catholic literature, differs from the Christian who is losing his faith. Some people move away from the Church because they find it increasingly difficult to accept that there is a redemptive mystery in human life. Life is identified by them simply with what they see; they find it impossible to believe in the mystery of God present to men. The third man differs also from the Christian who loses interest in the Church because he gives in to his selfish desires. A Christian may become so self-centred that the community of faith and love becomes a burden to him. He may stay away from the Church because he finds the Gospel a hard road to follow. Again the third man is different from the confused Christian who does not know what to believe anymore. Because of the changes in liturgy and doctrinal emphasis and because of the uncertainty in regard to much of traditional morality, some Catholics may simply be confused. They want to follow the Church but they no longer know exactly what this implies. The third man, as analysed by François Roustang, we conclude, is neither the unfaithful man, nor the selfish man, nor the confused man. Who, then, is he?

The third man wants to be faithful to the divine presence revealed in Christ and mediated in the Catholic Church. He wants to be sensitive to the Spirit who creates the Church. The third man, it seems to me, is an inevitable phenomenon accompanying the Church's entry into a new spiritual-cultural environment and the re-focusing of the Gospel which this entails. We have shown that Vatican II has begun to re-focus the self-identical Gospel and that the re-interpretation of the Church's teaching in the light of the new focus is a gradual process. While we pass through this process we are all more or less third men. As

Catholics we accept the Church's teaching, but as we adjust to the new focus of the Gospel, there are many doctrinal positions to which we are, at this time, unable to assign a clear meaning. These doctrinal positions were formulated with a reference to a previous focus. Because the focus has been shifted, these positions no longer make the sense they once did; and because the process of re-interpretation is a gradual one, it may happen that these positions cannot yet be related to the new focus. These positions seem to hang in the air. What is required is more reflection, more dialogue, more theological research, more vital engagement in Christian life. This will speed up the process of re-interpretation. In some important cases, what may be required is the endorsement of the re-interpretation by the ecclesiastical magisterium.

Let me give a simple example. The attitude of the Catholic Church to infant baptism made sense in terms of the restrictive understanding of Church. Baptism is man's saving contact with Jesus Christ, the one mediator. Children can be saved only through baptism. We thought, therefore, that it was a matter of great urgency to baptize babies that were dying, whether they came from Christian families or not. We thought that without baptism a child could not enter the glory of God. This doctrinal understanding determined the baptismal practise of the Church. Catholic priests, for instance, were not permitted to give liturgical burial to babies that had died without baptism, even when they came from Christian parents. Or, to extend the influence of baptism, Catholic hospitals would preform intra-uterine baptisms in cases where the life of the embryo was threatened before birth. Today, after Vatican II, the Church teaches that God is redemptively involved in human history. To be born into the human family means to be born into a sinful community and to become

203

a sinner oneself; at the same time, it means to belong to a community that has been oriented once for all toward divine salvation. To be human—in this history—means to be summoned to salvation. For this reason our attitude to baptism is bound to change. We no longer want to defend infant baptism in the Church on the theory that without it little babies are excluded from salvation. We no longer want to be over-anxious about the baptism of babies. A Catholic who is not theologically trained may not be able to express these insights in correct theological propositions; he may not be able to work out a theology which explains the positive meaning of infant baptism in the Church and at the same time acknowledges the salvation of babies who die without baptism. The old doctrinal position no longer makes sense to the Catholic; he no longer accepts the anxious practise of the past; at the same time he may not be able to re-interpret the old position in the light of the new focus and come to a satisfactory doctrinal position. He becomes a third man. This is a slight example of a phenomenon which is wide and reaches deeply into the doctrinal life of the Church.

I wish to mention in this connection that Charles Davis is not a third man. He left the Catholic Church and took up a doctrinal position against her. In the view of Charles Davis, a Catholic is ignoble and insincere if he puts a question mark behind a doctrinal position defined by the Catholic Church. He interprets such a question mark as a sign of doubt or disbelief. Such a Catholic, Davis feels, ought to leave the Catholic Church. In our view, the entry of the Church into a new spiritual-cultural environment leads to a re-focusing of the Gospel and to a process of re-interpreting traditional teaching in which open questions are removed only gradually. In this state of transition every Catholic is more or less a third man.

Let us return to the thesis of this chapter that the sociological model for the institutional life of the Open Church is the outer-oriented movement. We saw that a movement is characterized—and differs from a closed society—by the fact that people belong to it in various ways and varying intensities, according to their own choice. While the official concept of the Church, expressed in canon law and the diocesan-parochial structure, is still that of a closed society, the doctrinal development of Vatican II and the experience of the Catholic people have produced a shift in the sociological reality of the Church—a shift, we add, in keeping with her divinely given hierarchical structure. The widespread phenomenon of "the third man" makes the Church a movement in fact, even while this may not be acknowledged by the ecclesiastical government.

This leads us to the next characteristic of an outer-oriented movement. A movement is institutionally visible at the centre. A society, we have said, is visible in every one of its members. Since membership is clearly defined, the boundary lines of a society can be clearly drawn. Yet the social organization of a movement is visible only at the centre: the movement is visible in its regular meetings and the on-going committees that plan these meetings. A movement assumes clear and often powerful visibility when the people variously associated with it gather for different purposes: to affirm their self-identity as a movement, to strengthen one another, to discuss and decide orientation and policies, to be educated and to plan education, to meet one another and become friends, to exchange ideas and learn from the experience of others, and so forth. The movement is, therefore, an institution. Its institutional life is embodied in the meetings and the on-going committees responsible for them. At the same time, the institutional part of an outer-oriented movement may not be the place where it is most vitally concentrated. The movement is most itself in the exercise of its mission.

It seems to me that, also from this viewpoint, the sociological model of movement fits the post-conciliar Church. The Church is institutionally visible at its meetings, especially at worship; it is visible at the other meetings, be they decision-making or simply educational. The variety of ways in which Christians associate themselves with, and come to be, the Catholic Church does not make her what in the old Protestant-Catholic polemics was called an "invisible Church". Regarding the Church as a movement does not weaken her institutional character. It simply assigns the institution a different role in the total life of the Church. Institution in the Church are the meetings. The hierarchical ministry in apostolic succession—in association with other Christians according to the evolution of canon law—organizes, serves, and directs these meetings. The divinely appointed ministry exercises their authority in the teaching, worship, and policies of the Church—not, indeed, to enforce uniformity but to promote diversity in the unity of faith. The apostolic authority remains with the episcopal college (including papal primacy) to protect and enliven the tensions implicit in the Gospel between the local and the universal, and between past and present. The Church as outer-oriented movement preserves the apostolic authority at its institutional centre to achieve the doctrinal consensus, accepted by all, for the re-focusing of the Gospel in ever-new environments.

In the Church that has become movement the authority of the hierarchical ministry will have to do mainly with the establishment and formulation of consensus. It will be power to promote the Gospel. The Church of tomorrow will no longer understand the power which Jesus gave the apostles and which is exercised by her ministers in terms of jurisdiction over people. The people will associate themselves in the movement freely and responsibly, as they decide in the Spirit.

What will the Church look like if she becomes a movement? Here is an example. Let us assume that a large North American city has 40 parishes. Parish means closed society. A parish has geographical boundaries. The pastor is in charge of the parish; he is appointed over the people. Then let us imagine that instead of these 40 parishes we have 10 or 15 centres of Christian life, conveniently spread over the whole city, without any territorial rights. At these centres, worship is celebrated on Sundays and throughout the week. Every day there are activities of various kinds in which people can involve themselves. There are talks, discussion groups, action programmes, adult education, catechesis for children . . . the action at the centres can be shared in by people. It stimulates them, makes them ask important questions, impresses on them the meaning of faith, and encourages them to reach out for the answers to new questions. People involve themselves in what happens at these centres, as they choose. When they go there no one has authority over them. If they want to participate on the organizational level, they will be able to do so and eventually influence the making of policy regarding the centre. But what counts is not so much what happens at the centre but what happens in people's lives as the result of their contact with these centres.

What would happen if the Church became a movement visible at the centre? We may find that at first there may be a numerical decrease. At the same time, I believe that the effect of the centres on the lives of people would be greater and hence the total influence of the Church on the society, even though through fewer Catholics, would be greater. The Church would be able to influence the social conscience of the city; it would stimulate programmes of social reform, it would make people generally more sensitive to what is precious and important in life. The Church in this situation would not face the secular society as a spiritual replica of itself, the Church would not inspire people to become members of her own societies and organizations, the Church would enable Catholics to become more dedicated members of the secular society in which they live. The Church as movement would intensify the people's involvement in the life of society. Through conversation and common action, the Church would draw men more deeply into the mystery of redemption present in human life. And if the participation in the worship and the programmes at these centres makes people more alive and more sensitive to what is real in life, then others will join them in their faith and worship God in union with them. The whole movement will remain strong enough to exercise the mission that makes it Church.

There are signs that in the big cities the Church is already taking on the form of a movement, even though this is not yet acknowledged by the ecclesiastical government. Where in the cities do people become deeply involved in Catholic life? Where do they learn about Christ? Where do they meet one another and become friends? Where do they learn to assume wider responsibility in the community? It would be unrealistic to say that this is happening in the city parishes today. The Catholic life of a city is often mediated through other institutions. There may be a Catholic centre or school or college that reaches out for the public; there may be special pastors and groups of priests who organize pastoral projects. There may be radio programmes and religious news that touch people. There may be religious congregations or individual parishes that have an influence on people.

The vitality of Catholic life, the new ideas people have, the ardent aspirations they entertain, the social impact they have on society . . . these things are not communicated through the parish system in the big cities. Sociologically speaking, the Catholic Church in big cities is already becoming a movement.

If this observation is correct, then the effort of the ecclesiastical government must eventually turn to a totally new pastoral approach. What must be created are ways of involving people in thinking and acting as Christians. Radio and television may turn out to be major sources of grace in the community. What we need is not new institutions in which people can be assigned their place; what we need are words and actions that move people, educate them, and make them live out their new life in the secular society. To use the terminology of Marshall McLuhan, the Church must become a "cool" Church: it must become a medium that invites participation.

It seems to me that understanding the Church as movement is in harmony with the sacramental and collegial structure of the Church. Is it also in harmony with the teaching that Church is community? Since the community created by the Church extends beyond her boundaries to others it seems to me that the outer-oriented movement is the only sociological model that does justice to this inclusive character of the Church. The Church as movement makes people conscious of what community means in the lives of men. At the institutional centre of the Church, Christians learn the mystery of community in the eucharist and in the teaching of Christ; they learn this, not to form a closed community about the visible centres but, rather, to become community-creators themselves and move into society, the places where they live and work, to form community with people there. The Open Church is the community of the faithful; but more than that, it initiates Christians into the redemptive role of community in human life and renders them capable of being friends with others and of making the people with whom they live a community. The Open Church, moreover, is community because through Christians it seeks to reconcile the human race as a community of men who are open to one another and willing to promote the well-being of all. In this action God is graciously present to men.

We conclude that the new self-understanding of man has a profound effect on the institutional structure of the Catholic Church. There is some evidence that the Church is being transformed from a closed society into an outer-oriented movement. The Open Church is defined in terms of the whole human family and her role in it. The Open Church is no spiritual replica of the political society. She is a movement, visible at the institutional centre, involving people in various ways, according to their own choices. This will eventually demand an adaptation of the Church's sacramental and collegial structure. Yet throughout this transition the Church remains herself, once for all founded by God in Christ, and forever recreated by his living Word, in the identity of God's gift of himself to men.

Notes

INTRODUCTION

1. Of Blondel's vast philosophical work only one volume is available in English: *Letter on Apologetics and History of Dogma*, introd. by A. Dru and I. Trethowan, London, 1964. Cf. also *Correspondence. Pierre Teilhard de Chardin, Maurice Blondel*, New York, 1967. An excellent introduction to Blondel's work is H. Bouillard, *Blondel et le christianisme*, Paris, 1961.

2. The focus of Rahner's vast theological work is expressed in his article "Anthropologie," *Lexikon für Theologie und Kirche*, vol. 1. Cf. H. Vorgrimler, *Karl Rahner*, Glen Rock, 1965.

3. Cf. *Contraception and Holiness*, ed. by Archbishop T. Roberts, New York, 1964, pp. 311–344.

CHAPTER 1

1. So well known is the Catholic position of the past, even among men hardly acquainted with the Catholic Church, that references do not seem necessary. Celebrated among Christians is the rigid formulation of the exclusivist position by Pope Boniface VIII in the bull *Unam sanctam* promulgated in 1302 (cf. Denz.-S. 870). Modern formulations of the exclusivist position are found in Leo XIII's *Satis cognitum*, 1896, Pius XI's *Mortalium animos*, 1928, and Pius XII's *Mystici corporis*, 1943.

2. For a brief history of this expression and the literature dealing with it see B. Willems, "Who Belongs to the Church?", *Concilium*, vol. 1 (American ed.), pp. 131–151.

3. Pius XII strongly affirmed the identity between Church and Catholic Church. Cf. *Mystici corporis*, Denz.-S. 3802, and *Humani generis*, Denz. 2319. He insisted that there was no Spirit-created communion between Catholics and outsiders. "Those divided (from us) in faith and ecclesi-

astical government do not live in the one body of Christ nor do they live by Christ's one Spirit" (*Mystici corporis*).

4. See G. Baum, "The New Self-Understanding of the Roman Catholic Church at Vatican II," *The Church in the Modern World,* ed. by G. Johnston, Toronto, 1967, pp. 86–107.

5. For a doctrinal presentation of the local Church, see the *Dogmatic Constitution on the Church,* art. 26.

6. Cf. *Constitution on the Church,* arts. 3 and 11; *Constitution on the Sacred Liturgy,* arts. 2 and 33; *Decree on Ecumenism,* art. 15.

7. Art. 10.

8. Art. 22.

9. Art. 3.

10. Cf. *Constitution on the Church,* art. 15.

11. Cf. Baum, "The Ecclesial Reality of the Other Churches," *Concilium,* vol. 4, pp. 62–86.

12. *Constitution on the Church,* art. 9: "Israel according to the flesh, which wandered as an exile in the desert, was already called the Church of God."

13. *Declaration on the Relationship of the Church to Non-Christian Religions,* art. 4: "For the Church of Christ acknowledges that, according to the mystery of God's saving design, the beginning of her faith and election are already found among the patriarchs, Moses and the prophets. She professes that all who believe in Christ, Abraham's sons according to faith, are included on the same patriarch's call, and likewise that the salvation of the Church was mystically foreshadowed by the chosen people's exodus from the land of bondage."

14. *Constitution on the Church,* art. 16. Cf. also *Declaration on Non-Christians,* art. 4: "Nevertheless, according to the Apostle (Paul) the Jews still remain most dear to God because of (His promise to) their fathers, for He does not repent of the gifts He makes nor of the calls He issues."

15. Cf. Baum, "The Doctrinal Basis for the Jewish-Christian Dialogue," *The Month,* November 1967, pp. 232–245.

16. *Constitution on the Church,* art. 2. On the subject of God's grace in mankind also see *ibid.,* art. 16; *Dogmatic Constitution on Divine Revelation,* art. 3; *Pastoral Constitution on the Church in the Modern World,* arts. 16 and 22.

17. Art. 2.

18. *Ibid.*

19. Art. 11.

20. A vast effort of contemporary Catholic theology has given the doctrine of original sin a more central place in the understanding of man and his world. Cf. A.-M. Dubarle, *The Biblical Doctrine of Original Sin,* New

York, 1964; A. Hulsbosch, *God in Creation and Evolution*, New York, 1965; L. Ligier, *Péché d' Adam et péché du monde*, 2 vols., Paris, 1955/1961; P. de Rosa, *Christ and Original Sin*, Milwaukee, 1967; P. Schoonenberg, *God's World in the Making*, Pittsburgh, 1964; and *Man and Sin*, New York, 1966.

21. Rom. 5, 12–21.

22. Cf. A. Hulsbosch, *God in Creation and Evolution*, chs. 2, 4, 5, and 7, New York, 1965.

23. Rom. 7, 7–25.

24. Rom. 7, 19–20.

25. *Decretum de peccato originale*, can. 4, Denz.-S. 1514.

26. Cf. P. Schoonenberg, *Man and Sin*, New York, 1966, pp. 157–177.

27. Cf. Baum, "The New Self-Understanding of the Roman Catholic Church."

28. Art. 22.

29. Gen. 9, 1–17. Cf. G. von Rad, *Genesis, A Commentary*, Philadelphia, 1961, pp. 126–130.

30. In the Old Testament God manifested himself as the God of salvation. Faith in God, the creator, is an extension of faith in God, the redeemer. It was by reflecting on the covenant and God's redemptive presence in their history that the prophets in Israel came to acknowledge God as the maker of the world. Cf. G. von Rad, *Old Testament Theology*, vol. 1, New York, 1962, pp. 136–139. God is creator because he makes the world and its history now.

31. "But now says the Lord, who created you, O Jacob, and formed you, O Israel: Fear not, for I have redeemed you, I have called you by your name—you are mine" (Is. 43, 1). The soteriological understanding of creation is found especially in Second Isaiah but it is by no means confined to it. See Reinelt, "Schöpfung," *Handbuch theologischer Grundbegriffe*, vol. 2, Munich, 1963, pp. 494–500.

32. For references to the biblical teaching on Logos, see R. Schnackenburg's article, "Logos," *Lex. f. Theol. und Kirche* and for a presentation of Logos in the thology of antiquity, see G. L. Prestige, *God in Patristic Thought*, London, 1952, pp. 112–128.

33. Col. 1, 15–20.

34. Cf. R. Scroggs, *The Last Adam, A Study in Pauline Anthropology*, Philadelphia, 1966.

35. Thomas Aquinas teaches that divine grace is offered to man born into sin from the first moment of his conscious life. If man responds positively by orienting his life to the proper end his inherited sin is forgiven and he enters into the state of grace; if he rejects the offer and refuses to orient his life towards the proper end, as it is discernible by him at that

age, he confirms the inherited sin by his own mortal sin. See *Summa Theol.*, I–II, 89, 6.

36. For a detailed account of the change, see Baum, "The Ecclesial Reality of the Other Churches."

37. *Constitution on the Church*, art. 8. See also the commentary on this article by A. Grillmeier, "Das Zweite Vatikanische Konzil," vol. 1, *Lex. f. Theol. und Kirche.*

38. After naming the gifts which build up and give life to the Churches, the Decree concludes, "It follows that the separated Churches and communities as such, though we believe them to suffer from the defects already mentioned, have been by no means deprived of significance and importance in the mystery of salvation. For the Spirit of Christ has not refrained from using them as means of salvation which derive their efficacy from the fullness of grace and truth entrusted to the Catholic Church" (art. 3).

39. *Ibid.*

40. *Ibid.*

41. For brief statements of their positions see K. Rahner, "On the Possibility of Faith Today," *Theological Investigations*, vol. 5, and E. Schillebeeckx, "The Church and Mankind," *Concilium*, vol. 1, pp. 69–102.

CHAPTER 2

1. *A Question of Conscience*, New York, 1967, pp. 64–67.

2. *Ibid.*, p. 65.

3. *Ibid.*, p. 73.

4. *Ibid.*, p. 75.

5. *Ibid.*, pp. 99–117.

6. *Ibid.*, p. 99.

7. *Ibid.*, p. 113.

8. *Ibid.*, pp. 76–92.

9. *Ibid.*, p. 79.

10. "Trial by Laicization," *The Commonweal* 87, December 8, 1967, pp. 328–331.

11. *A Question of Conscience*, p. 89.

12. *Ibid.*, p. 90.

13. Paris, 1950.

14. *Is the New Testament Anti-Semitic?* (rev. ed. of *The Jews and the Gospel*), New York, 1965.

15. Cf. Jn. 9, 41.

16. Is. 6, 10. Cf. Mt. 13, 14 and Jn. 12, 40.

17. Cf. Mt. 23, 5–9.

18. Cf. Acts 13, 45. The "jealousy" of the synagogue is a recurring theme in the writings of Luke. Cf. Baum, *Is the New Testament Anti-Semitic?*, pp. 213–214.

19. To bridge the cultural gap between Christians the Church imposed certain minimal rules on Gentile Christians. Cf. Acts 15, 28–29.

20. Cf. Mk. 7, 8 and Mt. 15, 3.

21. Art. 6.

22. H. Küng, *Die Kirche,* Freiburg, 1967, pp. 37–43.

23. Cf. *The University Game,* ed. Adelman and Lee, Toronto, 1968.

24. I here draw on the thought of Aarne Siirala. See his *The Voice of Illness,* Philadelphia, 1964.

25. "Relationship of Church and World in the Light of a Political Theology," *Theology of Renewal,* Proceedings of the Congress on the Theology of the Church, Centenary of Canada, 1867–1967, vol. II: *Renewal of Religious Structures,* New York, 1968. Cf. *The Ecumenist,* 5, September/October 1967, p. 86.

26. *Ibid.*

CHAPTER 3

1. See Küng, *op. cit.,* pp. 410–425.

2. For a wider use of the word "apostle," see Acts 13, 3; 14, 4; Rom. 16, 7; 1 Cor. 12, 28; 15, 7–9; 2 Cor. 8, 23; 11, 5; Phil. 2, 25.

3. "The development of the strictly doctrinal concept of the apostles was not the extension of a narrow concept (the Twelve) to a wider one (the authoritative witnesses of Christ), but the restriction of a wider concept to the Twelve (and possibly, Paul)." Küng, *op. cit.,* p. 416.

4. *Ibid.,* p. 422.

5. 1 Cor. 12, 28.

6. Küng, *op. cit.,* pp. 467–469.

7. *Ibid.,* p. 483.

8. *Ibid.,* p. 484.

9. *Ibid.,* pp. 492–495.

10. Denz.-S. 1776.

11. *Constitution on the Church,* art. 28.

12. For a discussion of the recent studies on "Frühkatholizismus" in the New Testament, see Küng, *Structures of the Church,* New York, 1964, pp. 152–169.

13. "The preaching of the Church, like the entire Christian religion, must be nourished and ruled by the Sacred Scriptures." *Constitution on Revelation,* art. 21.

14. Cf. R. Adolfs, *The Grave of God,* New York, 1967.

15. Cf. Küng, "The Charismatic Structure of the Church," *Concilium,* vol. 4, pp. 41–61.

16. Cf. A. Kolping, "Notae Ecclesiae," *Lex. f. Theol. u. Kirche,* vol. 6.

17. Cf. O. Karrer, *Peter and the Church,* New York, 1963; A. Voegtle, "Petrus," *Lex. f. Theol. u. Kirche,* vol. 8; B. Rigaux, "St. Peter in Contemporary Exegesis," *Concilium,* vol. 27, pp. 147–179.

CHAPTER 4

1. See above, pp. 50–51.

2. *America,* January 6, 1968, pp. 14–15.

3. *Ibid.*

4. *The Church Against Itself,* New York, 1967, pp. 157–158.

5. On this theological basis we are able to reaffirm—albeit in a different light—everything the ecclesiastical magisterium of the 19th century proposed regarding the "objectivity" of the Christian foundation.

6. Cf. *The Fourth World Conference on Faith and Order,* Montreal, 1963, London, 1964, pp. 16–17.

7. Denz.-S. 3061.

8. Cf. J. P. Torrell, *La théologie de l'épiscopat au premier Concile du Vatican,* Paris, 1961, pp. 149–158; G. Dejaifve, *Pape et évêques au premier Concile du Vatican,* Brussels, 1961, pp. 81–91.

9. "While preserving unity in essentials let everyone in the Church, according to the office entrusted to him, preserve a proper freedom in the various forms of the spiritual life and discipline, in the variety of liturgical rites and even in the theological elaborations of revealed truth." *Decree on Eucumenism,* art. 4. The canonical, liturgical and theological pluralism in the Church is vigorously affirmed in regard to the traditions of East and West. Cf. *ibid.,* arts. 16–17. Pluralism in the Catholic Church is the subject of several essays in *Theology of Renewal,* 2 vols. For references, see *The Ecumenist,* 5, September/October 1967, pp. 81–85.

10. When I speak of doctrinal consensus I do not have in mind a total agreement on all points of doctrine and values of life. More than once I have acknowledged the need for a theological pluralism in the Catholic Church. The doctrinal consensus of which I speak has to do, as we shall see below, with the focus of the Gospel and the Church's understanding of her mission.

11. *New Blackfriars,* 48, January 1967, pp. 170–171.

12. "We know that nowadays certain trends of thought which still describe themselves as Catholic attempt to attribute a priority in the normative formulation of the truths of faith, to the community of the

faithful." Pope Paul, VI's speech on February 22, 1967, quoted in the *National Catholic Reporter,* March 1, 1967. Cf. his speech on January 11, 1967, quoted in the *National Catholic Reporter,* January 19, 1967.

13. Jude 3.

14. New York, 1960, pp. 57–63.

15. *Ibid.,* Part II: "Doctrinal Development Viewed Relatively to Doctrinal Corruptions", pp. 175–418.

16. A good survey of the theological literature on doctrinal devolopment is H. Hammans, "Recent Catholic Views on the Development of Dogma", *Concilium,* vol. 21, pp. 109–131. This survey is based on the large work by the same author, *Die neueren katholischen Erklärungen der Dogmenentwicklung,* Essen, 1965, and K. Rahner/K. Lehmann, *Mysterium Salutis,* vol. I, Einsiedeln, 1965, pp. 727–787.

17. Here, too, Blondel has been the first to insist that dogmas are not produced by reflection on given texts; they are expressions of a continuing reality tested by the experience of life. Cf. Blondel's essay "History and Dogma", *Letter on Apologetics and History of Dogma.* For an evaluation of Blondel and a discussion of his influence—"leider bis heute systematisch viel zu wenig beachtet" —see Rahner/Lehmann, *Mysterium Salutis,* p. 752.

18. Cf. Baum, "Vatican II's Constitution on Divine Revelation", *Theological Studies,* 28, 1967, pp. 51–75, esp. 61–64; P. van Leeuwen, "The Dogmatic Constitution on Divine Revelation" and L. Bakker, "What is Man's Place in Divine Revelation?", *Concilium,* vol. 21, pp. 5–38.

19. New York, 1967, p. 6.

20. *Constitution on the Church in the Modern World,* art. 44.

21. "Ideas are appearing in the fields of exegesis and theology which have their origin in certain bold but misleading philosophical theories and which cast doubt upon or narrow down the full meaning of the truths which the Church has taught with her rightful authority. There is a pretense that religion must be adapted to the contemporary mind." Pope Paul VI, "Exhortation on the 19th Centenary of the Martyrdom of SS. Peter and Paul," *The Pope Speaks,* 12, 1967, p. 141.

22. Art. 4.

23. *Ibid.*

24. Art. 5

25. *Ibid.*

26. "Signs of the times" was an expression frequently used by Pope John XXIII, especially in his encyclical *Pacem in terris.* Cf. M. Vanhengel/J. Peters, "Signs of the Times", *Concilium,* vol. 25, pp. 143–152.

27. *Constitution on the Church in the Modern World,* art. 11.

28. *Ibid.,* art. 4.

29. This thought is examined by M.-D. Chenu in his essay "The History of Salvation and the Historicity of Man in the Renewal of Theology",

Theology of Renewal, vol. 1: *Renewal of Religious Thought.* His conclusions are summarized in *The Ecumenist,* 5, September/October 1967, pp. 91–92. Chenu writes (as quoted in *The Ecumenist*), "The Church is in the world of time . . . She is here as the expression and interpretation of the very truth of the revealed data. The Word of God speaks today in the hierarchical and magisterial community in which it is the living architect. Thus we are not concerned with an 'adaptation' of the Word of God conceived in abstract purity. We are not dressing up and stripping abstract formulas. It is a rereading of Scripture that progressively reveals its appropriate significance in each generation of the Church, thanks to the light which the present moment throws upon the past when past and present confront each other, open to the future. It is a permanent reinterpretation, within the regulating community and as conditioned by the magisterium, of truths within the unchangeable identity of their intentionality. . . . It is wrong for the theologian to isolate, or 'put into parentheses' as it were, contemporary thought in order first to determine exactly what has been revealed and only then, as a second step, to translate it into contemporary language." According to Chenu doctrinal renewal must always be an original, creative, Spirit-produced reformulation of the Gospel in a new age, using the language proper to the experience of contemporary life. Chenu thinks that the first requirement in this process is the sensitivity of Christians to the presence and action of God in history.

30. Arts. 23–32.

31. "This Vatican Council proclaims the highest destiny of man and champions the divine seed which has been sown in him. It offers to mankind the most honest assistance of the Church in fostering that brotherhood of all men which corresponds to this destiny of theirs. Inspired by no earthly ambition the Church seeks but a single goal: to carry forward the work of Christ under the lead of the befriending Spirit" (art. 3). The common brotherhood of man in the selfsame destiny and the Church's task of intensifying this brotherhood in the Spirit is acknowledged throughout this Constitution.

32. The recent development in the theological understanding of the word "brother" has not yet been studied. For useful references see Willems, "Who Belongs to the Church?", *Concilium,* vol. 1, pp. 131–151.

33. For a totally negative evaluation of the ecumenical movement on the part of the ecclesiastical authorities, see Pope Pius XI's encyclical *Mortalium animos,* 1928.

34. *The Future of Belief,* New York, 1966, pp. 96–121.

CHAPTER 5

1. *A Question of Conscience,* pp. 192–209.

2. "Restlessness in the Church", *The Ecumenist,* 5, March/April 1967, pp. 33–36.

3. Cf. *Constitution on the Church,* arts. 2 and 16; *Constitution on the Church in the Modern World,* arts. 16 and 22.

4. *Constitution on the Church in the Modern World,* art. 5.

5. Cf. J. Ratzinger, "The Pastoral Implications of Episcopal Collegiality", *Concilium,* vol. 1, pp. 39–68.

6. On the participation of the clergy and laity in the government of the diocese, see *Decree on the Bishops' Pastoral Office in the Church,* art. 27.

7. *Constitution on the Church,* art. 28. See Baum, "The Ministerial Priesthood," *Ecumenical Theology No. 2,* New York, 1967, pp. 230–238.

8. *Decree on Religious Life,* art. 4.

9. Cf. the proceedings of the Canon Law Society of America, 1965, 1966 and 1967. Cf also F. Klostermann, "Structures of the Church of Tomorrow", IDO-C (North America) 1967, doss. 28, 29.

10. Cf. H. Heimerl, "Outline of a Constitution for the Church," *Concilium,* vol. 28, pp. 59–68, and the conclusions of the Canon Law Society of America, 1967, "Towards Constitutional Development in the Church", IDO-C (North America) 1968, doss. 1.

11. *Decree on the Church's Missionary Activity,* art. 3: "This universal design of God for the salvation of the human race is not carried out exclusively with a kind of secrecy in the souls of men. Nor is it achieved merely through those multiple endeavors, including religious ones, by which men search for God . . . For these attempts need to be enlightened and purified, even though, through the kind disposition of divine providence, they may sometimes serve as guidance toward the true God or as a preparation for the Gospel".

12. *Christus,* 13, 1966, 561–567. Cf. M. West, "Testimony of a 20th Century Catholic", *America,* December 2, 1967, p. 681.

Index

221